The
Louisville
Review

Number 92
Fall/Winter 2022

Get ready for *The Louisville Review*'s

NATIONAL POETRY BOOK CONTEST!

In 2023 *The Louisville Review* and Fleur-de-Lis Press will announce a NEW National Poetry Book Contest, a first-book poetry contest open to writers in the United States.

TLR's first contest as an independent journal is made possible by a generous grant from the Snowy Owl Foundation.

THE LOUISVILLE REVIEW

Editor	Sena Jeter Naslund
Associate Editor	Flora K. Schildknecht
Managing Editor	Amy Foos Kapoor
Guest Poetry Editors	Debra Kang Dean, Wanda Fries
Guest Fiction Editor	Drēma Drudge
Cornerstone Editor	Betsy Woods
Technical Director	Ron Schildknecht
Financial Director	John Morgan

TLR publishes two volumes each year. Visit our website for complete guidelines, back issues, subscriptions, and more: www.louisvillereview.org.

Like us on Facebook for up to date information about each issue, news on contributors, etc.: www.facebook.com/TheLouisvilleReview. Follow us on Twitter @TheLouRev.

Questions? Please note our email and mailing addresses:

managingeditor@louisvillereview.org.

The Louisville Review Corp.
1436 St. James Court #1
Louisville, Kentucky 40208

This issue: $10 ppd
Sample copy: $5 ppd
Subscriptions: One year, $18; two years, $36; three years, $54 plus $2 shipping.
Subscribers outside the United States please add $35/year for shipping.

Text and cover printed in the United States. Cover design by Jonathan Weinert.

Cover artwork, Ying Kit Chan, *Turbulence*, 2022, acrylic and plastic on wood, 36 x 27 inches (91 x 69 cm). Photo courtesy of the artist.

The Kentucky Arts Council, the state arts agency, provides American Rescue Plan funds to The Louisville Review Corporation with federal funding from the National Endowment of the Arts. *The Louisville Review* is a not-for-profit publication.

The Louisville Review Corporation is a member of the Community of Literary Magazines and Presses.

We open this issue with a poem, "**Poetry Ought to be Able to Comprehend the World**," by the late poet Frederick Smock (1954-2022), a Kentucky Poet Laureate, a friend and supporter of *The Louisville Review* for decades, and guest poetry editor of our recent forty-fifth anniversary issue #90. Frederick Smock's impact on the Kentucky literary landscape cannot be overstated, and his sudden loss earlier this year reverberates deeply—see Editor Sena Jeter Naslund's tribute, "In Remembrance of Frederick Smock, a Kentucky Poet Laureate," and Tony O'Keeffe's poem, "Mourning."

The directive in the title of Smock's poem, drawn from Robert Hass' poem "State of the Planet" (1999), resonates with the fullness and scope of the situations engaged in *TLR* #92. The work in this issue collectively asserts that poetry, fiction, prose, and art can and indeed must be able to "comprehend the world," in all its complexity. The art featured on the cover, *Turbulence*, a three-dimensional painting by Ying Kit Chan, gestures toward some of that complexity by engaging man-made climate catastrophe; the illuminating "Essay on Cover Art: *Turbulence*" by Chris Reitz connects the formal elements of Chan's painting to the conflicting worldviews that contribute to climate precarity.

In keeping with *TLR*'s ongoing endeavors to embrace perspectives and writers from outside the US more fully, we are delighted to present new poems from Chinese poet and artist Congxia Ma, both in the original Chinese script and in English translation. In the fiction in this issue readers will encounter a wide gamut of concerns and locales, from the terror of being young and female in pre-Roe v. Wade small-town America in Patricia Foster's "That Life," to the atrocity of nuclear devastation in Hiroshima in David Wilde's "The Red Oleander," to the joys of serendipitous encounters in the streets of Istanbul in Sarah Martin's "Magic Birthday."

Dianne Aprile's nonfiction essay "Keeping Records" was previously published in *TLR* #66, and Aprile revised the piece to reflect her recent move back to Louisville, KY, from Seattle; this updated essay nimbly takes readers on a journey through generations and decades. For an extraplanetary journey, readers can travel through the solar system in "Mandorla Golry," an excerpt from Robert Eric Shoemaker's recently completed serial poem, *A Planetary Spell*, an exploration of queerness and magical poetics. Both Aprile and Shoemaker read their work this summer at Voice & Vision, an annual summer reading series presented by 21c Museum Hotel in Louisville in partnership with Spalding University's

Naslund-Mann Graduate School of Writing and *The Louisville Review*; Voice & Vision is coordinated by *TLR*'s Managing Editor, Amy Foos Kapoor.

In the coming months, stay on the lookout for the announcement of our new **National Poetry Book Contest**, a first-book poetry contest open to writers in the US. *TLR*'s first iteration of the contest as an independent journal is made possible by a generous grant from the Snowy Owl Foundation.

The work we do at *TLR* would not be possible without the essential contributions of our guest editors for each issue, and I extend our heartfelt thanks to our guest poetry editors, who along with myself, selected the poetry for this issue of *TLR*:

Totem: America, **Debra Kang Dean**'s third book of poetry, was shortlisted for the Indiana Authors Award in Poetry in 2020. In addition to her books of poetry, she has published two prize-winning chapbooks and, with Russ Kesler, a chapbook of renku. Recent publications include poems in *They Rise Like a Wave: An Anthology of Asian American Women Poets* and *The World I Leave You: Asian American Poets on Faith and Spirit* as well as reviews of Kaveh Akbar's *Pilgrim Bell* and of Cyrus Cassells' *The World That the Shooter Left Us*. She is on the poetry faculty of Spalding University's Naslund-Mann Graduate School of Writing.

Wanda Fries lives in Kentucky and has recently retired from full-time teaching. She has written two novels, a collection of short stories, and a collection of poetry, *Cassandra among the Greeks*. Her stories and poems have appeared over the years in various magazines and journals.

Likewise, I extend our deep gratitude to our guest fiction editor, who along with Editor Sena Jeter Naslund, selected the fiction for this issue:

Drēma Drudge is the award-winning author of the novel *Victorine*. She graduated from the Naslund-Mann Graduate School of Writing with an MFA degree. She and her husband, musician and writer Barry Drudge, have two grown children and live in a small town in Indiana. They host the podcast MFA Payday. Learn more about Drēma and get a free story at: www.dremadrudge.com.

And many thanks to **Betsy Woods**, for continuing to help *TLR* showcase original poetry from young writers in the US and beyond as Editor of our Cornerstone section of poetry by writers in grades K-12.

—Flora K. Schildknecht, Associate Editor

TABLE OF CONTENTS

CORNERSTONE
work by writers K-12

Sena Jeter Naslund

In Remembrance of Frederick Smock, a Kentucky Poet Laureate

When I first came to teach at the University of Louisville in the early 1970's, I was immediately impressed by the quality of both undergraduate English majors and graduate students, who were so welcoming to me and appreciative of my efforts to affirm their talents and to help them with creative writing theses at the Master's level. It's with a sense of great loss that I write now, more than fifty years later, of the unexpected death of poet Frederick Smock, one of those gifted and quietly ambitious students.

Poetry and contemporary literature became the cornerstone of Fred's working life as a college teacher and as editor of the amazing literary magazine *The American Voice*, featuring work by writers in both North and South America. Fred began teaching at Bellarmine University in Louisville in 1997. In addition to having served as a departmental chair of English at Bellarmine, in recent years he served as Director of Creative Writing at Bellarmine and created the creative writing minor.

Back in the early 1970's Fred was one of the first students who came to my office wanting guidance for a Master's thesis consisting of his original poems. It was working with Fred that first made me realize how gifted and sincere these students were in their desire to create poems of value, expressive and true. Often short capsules of moments intensely or surprising experienced, Fred's poems opened doors for the reader in new and significant ways. Each came as a gift. They were often poems of private moments of discoveries in nature, sometimes of shared moments experienced in a way that illumined an aspect of another person; perhaps I should say his poems often offered a moment of revelation, but one without trumpets. Those were quiet moments, intimate ones, like a glance, after which one is never again quite the same. I was delighted and privileged to publish his poems many times in *The Louisville Review*.

Frederick Smock had a rare talent for making the poem a temporal creation, like music. And his poetry had, at the same time, a suggestion of space, of narrowing the distance between writer and reader. You, the reader, moved closer to him, stepped into his world for a moment, at his invitation. And came away from his world a richer, more sensitive, more inclusive person yourself. I wish we could have him back.

Because I feel sure that it would make him smile for you to visit his work now, let me mention a few of Frederick Smock's many books, some available from Larkspur Press, in Monterey, Kentucky, a press that is literally hand set, hand printed, and hand bound.

> *Book of Earthly Delights*, Larkspur Press
> *The Blue Hour*, Larkspur Press
> *Gardencourt*, Larkspur Press
> *Guest House*, Larkspur Press
> *The Good Life*, Larkspur Press
> *The Bounteous World*, Broadstone Books
> *Pax Intrantibus: A Meditation on the Poetry of Thomas Merton*,
> Broadstone Books
> *Images in Black, Continuous*, Regina Derieva,
> translated by Frederick Smock, M-Graphics Publishing

Poetry

Frederick Smock

The sun wakes us, tip-
toeing into our room, making
no sound. We wake like
flowers, turning, before they know it,
toward the light.

Frederick Smock

Poetry Ought to be Able to Comprehend the World

For Bob Korn

Is, more or less, a line in a poem by Robert Haas,
whom we were reading earlier today.
And now we are considering just how it is
that moss in Patagonia subsists on a diet of fog.
That lichen in the Arctic eats granite.
That our own bodies are heavenly: star-matter;
they feel the shifts in the night.
You slide your left leg under mine.
We are eating Chinese take-out at the foot of the bed,
dribbling soy sauce onto a dynasty roll.
In the half-light of dusk, through a west-
facing window, the bright burn of Venus shines
above the low arc of earth-light.
A body vaguely moving westward with the night.
It seems that science might be the new poetry,
ever since Niels Bohr gave us the metaphor of the atom.
(Is that really what an atom looks like,
Kunitz asked, or might it be just a symbol
of what we know only thus far?)
My father, who studied x-rays for a living,
always said his work was an art—the divination of bones—
an atomic flashlight at play in the ossuary
of the body, where a hairline shadow could be
a fracture or just a hairline shadow. Hard to say,
sometimes. Interpretation is everything. E.g.,
out west, the Nazca plate slides east three inches
per year, pretty fast in geological terms,
wrecking houses and cathedrals as it goes...
It is making steady progress, though toward *what*
we cannot say.

Frederick Smock

Solitude of the poet writing.
Solitude of the reader reading.
Between these two solitudes
runs a deep river
running fast with electric blue fishes.

Tony O'Keeffe

MOURNING

For Fred Smock

How bitter, that the word should echo dawn:
Morning, maker of light, day's first measure.
Outside my window the green trees rustle
As with a sound announcing autumn,
Trembling, as if within the chill ahead.
Autumn. If only autumn.

Not unexpected winter, come too soon,
Arriving with its freight of sorrow.
How quick the frail tapestry of a life
Can be torn, unwound, its fair forms undone.

So premature, his terrible exit.
And now:

All the gleaming words to be—unwritten.
The sweet pleasures of a simple day.
A lover's sigh, as sunset comes.
Every dim mist of morning.
Every wave heard breaking.
Each winter's crisp bite.
Each sudden line.
Poem born.
Himself.

Lost.

Millard Dunn

A LATE CONVERSATION

"When I was younger," the old man said,
"Thoughts would race around in my brain,
Faster sometimes than I could follow them.
Always looking for connections."
"And now?" his wife asks, hoping
He will be honest with her, as always.
        "Now my brain is a vast marsh
With a cold front coming. My thoughts
Wander through this marsh with no
Idea where they're going, and can't
Remember where they've been.
The names of people I've known for years,
Their faces, where I knew them, and what
We did together are disappearing under
The water, getting lost in the mud
I'm stuck in, and you," he said,
"Are the bright sail far ahead of me
In the sunlight. I can't remember all
The beautiful places you've taken me."
"I can," she said. "Take my hand."

Congxia Ma

REMEMBERING MY GRANDMOTHER

马丛霞
念祖母

初夏，泥巴，蒲扇，华发
深秋，月下，神话，庄稼 ……

湮没于您的皱纹，
发白于我的记忆。

您煨的温暖丝丝散去，
无视我的哀求，
悄然且决绝，
像不曾存在。

我知道，
我身体的一部分已随你而去。

Congxia Ma

REMEMBERING MY GRANDMOTHER

Early summer, wet muddy ground, palm leaf fan, gray hair,
Deep autumn, under the moonlight, fairy tales, harvested crops . . .

Buried in your wrinkles,
Slowly vanishing in my memory.

Your affection for me is gradually fading away,
Ignoring my pleas,
quietly and resolutely,
as if your love never existed.

I realize,
pieces of myself died with you.

translated from Chinese by the author and Ying Kit Chan

Congxia Ma

THE FLÂNEUR

马丛霞
游荡者

于摆脱中跌坠，
这不是必由之路吗？
瀑布的另一端，遥不可及，
也许永不可及。
意识的空白处，可会有新景？

拿往昔来填塞吧！
决然煅下了什么呢？
在回忆里游荡吧！
囚禁我的竟是我。

高明的你呀。

Congxia Ma

THE FLÂNEUR

Falling into the abyss while trying to break free,
Isn't it my inescapable destiny?
The end of this descent seems so far away,
maybe I will never stop sinking.
Can new vistas emerge from this void of consciousness?

I fill in the emptiness with the past,
What are the consequences of my determination?
Wandering in my own memory!
It was I who imprisoned myself.

How crafty you are!

translated from Chinese by the author and Ying Kit Chan

Daisy Bassen

THIS IS A LOVE POEM IF YOU SQUINT HARD ENOUGH

I hope you know
That when I say
I hope, I don't;
Nothing rises within
Me, nothing peers out
From a corner, nothing
Takes hold of me
Like the labor of birth,
The ease of a wanted
Conception. I've given
Up already, assuming
The worst: ignorance
Or a positive rejection
With the nerveless force
Of jostling magnets.

I hope you know
Something I imagine
Nestled in your mind
As the iron globe
Onion-layered at the earth's
Impossible depth, spinning
And still, the rooted origin
Of auroras, an ungrown green
North and south, egalitarian
In its display, most generous
When it's winter, when
We're so very cold.

Daisy Bassen

You Should Be Flattered

I don't follow most men.
Which I admit isn't a death-blow to the patriarchy,
Or even grabbing it by the balls and twisting,
Squeeze the juice, that's what the instructor called out
In women's self-defense class, where we were taught
Not to get in the car and to scream with keys
In our hands like Wolverine's claws. *Little one's loud,*
The instructor said and recorded it, to share with women
Who weren't, so I could be the see-one, an exemplar
Of resistance or at least of making someone turn around
If I'd been drafted as a victim, my turn now
To wonder if this was it, it being a point of no return,
The before and after that would start the timeline
For a PTSD diagnosis if things went sort-of my way.
I remember screaming. I remember how it felt to hit
The note that was wordless, right on pitch, *Ave Maria*
In my key, and the dreamy suspicion I'd fail in the clutch,
Mouth open like Ariel with her leggy regrets, her raw deal,
Because there were only so many hours to practice
Screaming before we had to leave so Zumba could start,
Another set of lithe girls in the mirror. Our teacher's name
Meant beautiful, you can decide in what language.

I would have followed her to the ends of the earth.

But she drove away in a grey sedan and this was the past,
When you couldn't find someone online
And fancy yourself an entourage. There was only the morning
And the air that had been screamed into, hospitable to terror
And poetry readings, neutral as Switzerland always claimed to be.

Kristin Camitta Zimet

TAXONOMY

Trout lily, owl moth, leopard frog:
names dip and leap, under and over
category walls. Forms commingle.
Fish crow burrows air, mole cricket
breaststrokes soil, fox grape snakes up
turkey oak. One thing tries on the next,
plays fast and loose with hybrids
and chimeras. On the rocks, the fungi
go to bed with algae and each other.
Have I got you grinning, can you grin,
now that from solid you've turned into
plasma, even less, to dead, to nothing?

But if labels fail, you are here, nowhere,
everywhere. In that dented canoe
we rocked among the reeds, making
our firstborn. When you swam into me,
that was for keeps. Some of your T cells
crossed into my blood. I'm carrying
your history, even your DNA. Call it
another way to marry. It takes work,
undoing the divide, when every tag
says widow, says bereaved. And then
I flow back into you, into us, the way
I slip down an embankment into sleep.

Kristin Camitta Zimet

CANOE

No longer will the waters
rock you, the patched shell
float. Gone to shallows,
shingle cutting keel, you
splashed in at this cove,
this hardbottom landing.

Your every breath a scrape.
You are dragging the canoe
up a gravel slope, hull rattling,
fingers cramped, chest rough.
Pausing, straining, you fight
the hauled-out body, balking
on its rope—the small breasts,
slim hips, skim-milk frame
I thought I would grow into.

My own breath insists—
slippery wash, careless slide—
blows into rooms in my chest,
giving and giving. Made to take,
greedy to live, I suckle air,
surprised as a baby at the leap
from cord to lungs. Pull, push,
I try to breathe for you, I can't
not try, Mommy, I can't—

But you never stopped for
nonsense. You are far ahead.
Gravel gives way to grass.
Dropping the enormous weight
of meager flesh, you stand,
straighten above yourself.

Elya Braden

{MENO/PAUSE}

These are the words we never say
    to each other:
        You are no longer a woman.
Hauling our empty rucksacks
    beneath our lungs, time no longer striding
        with the tides, only a river of days,
unbloodied, uncounted.
    We stand before the fire.
        We sleep beneath the ice.
This is the journey unforetold
    on any map. The land of sea dragons
        and monsters heaving in the great beyond.
We carry our bones like kindling, ready
    to break, ready to feed our daughters'
        fire. Each morning, the mirror greets us
with the mask of our unbecoming. Where
    do we find ourselves in this atlas of gullies
        and crevasses? What God ordained
we would crumple into our future?
    What God gilded our mouths in silence, forbade
        us from rescuing our sisters with song and shine.
The moon no longer guides us through
    the night. What can we do but pray
        our own stars into the dark,
construct our own constellations: Sarah, 90, laughing,
    lifting her wilted breast to her greedy miracle;
        Rebecca scooping water from a well;
Leah and Rachel, two points of a triangle,
    bright with jealousy and deceit. Oh, great
        mothers, what can you teach us to love
this barren parade of days? *Crone*, once a word
    of blessing, of wisdom scraped from earth
        and plucked from branches, now a curse, not

Eve's curse, but the curse of forgetting,
    of learning to live again in the desert
        of the forgotten.

Karen McAferty Morris

FIGS

Rosy figs in a basket
of woven willow, fresh-ripe in sultry July,
on the fallen ones, early morning bee scouts
crawl and hover over the juice
of split skins.

The harvested ones are firm.
Do not hide them all away like those plums
Williams discovered in the icebox.

Bite into them now, or slit them, taste the dense
moist flesh, no tame apple texture
or smooth peach or grape,
intricate, exotic, a rich delicate sweetcrunch,
your chin shining.

Write no note asking forgiveness.
From bud to flower, swelling and billowing
through daytime hours of lavish cicada rattle,
nights of thick ginger lily and jasmine perfume,
they were formed for you, be grateful
and greedy.

Juan Pablo Mobili

CHRIST IN THE RAIN

> *How is it I can never find*
> *Or call to mind*
> *One image of Christ walking slowly in the rain*
> *—Donald Revell*

He pulls up the collar of his raincoat,
no hat, a few days' dark stubble, looking
at his likeness gleaming on the sidewalk.

From the resignation that lightly shapes his shoulders
I'd surmise he's coming from a meeting in the basement
of a church, more troubled than uplifted.

He looks weary, still in his thirties,
and the rain does not seem to distract him
from his longing.

I doubt the rain will ever tempt him
to forsake his faith, but you can't be sure,
you cannot be a saint without a body.

Angie Macri

TERMINAL SPIKES

The false dragonhead stood
tall as a child
on the prairie named for a cemetery.
See the grave demanding
its way even here
where the sky goes on forever?
Not ever having seen a dragon,

the child has no way to know
if it's truly false
or just so called.
Some prefer its other name,
obedient plant
because it stays when pushed down.
A woman has been found

without hands, another without tongue.
They move into town,
rescued, poor creatures
say some, others with more suspicion,
too close to the devil
and wouldn't back down.
The town was named long ago for a poem

found to be false,
not some ancient translation
but old songs a man took and spun
into a land where people kill
what they love, where people die
of joy and broken hearts, a land the child
has already begun to know.

Joe Schmidt

ELEGY FOR A TURKISH COMMUNIST

Uncle Ahmet waited for the revolution,
like many good communists,
but it never came, not to Turkey.
His brother went to prison for a poem in a leftist paper.
So Uncle Ahmet worked for his father's trucking company.
He traveled to Tblisi and Yerevan.
In place of the revolution, there was *rakı*,
or vodka, toasts and songs for the Turkish Republic.
His wife and children left him, but there was never a divorce.
Later he inherited a walnut orchard, wealth which endeared him
to relatives who had long before disposed of him.
Later still, a pensioner, he wandered the mazes of Gaziantep,
smoked bootleg Armenian cigarettes, watched documentaries
about shamanism—*original religion*, he called it.
When he accepted that his niece married me, an American,
he demanded a colt pistol and bottle of Kentucky bourbon.

Uncle Ahmet had a view of the Syrian border from his room
at the oncology hospital. Red arid hills and no sign of the war.
Every night the purple twilight and the man dying beside him,
a half living ghost with paper flesh on bones of wire.
Uncle Ahmet was a pest to the nurses, so they moved him away
from the window, and he took his chemo drip staring at a wall.
That summer a crowd of old women prayed at Uncle Ahmet's funeral.
Many mourned him who had nothing good to say about him in life.
His wife and adult children returned to claim his walnut orchard.

Wendy Taylor Carlisle

TAROT

I will show you fear in a handful of dust.
    —*T. S. Eliot*

1. The Drowned Phoenician Sailor
A canoe. Metal, I think. And I kept saying "stop giving me orders, I'll freeze up," but he didn't stop. Until the canoe capsized. It was an accident. I was wet and laughing. I was eighteen. It was never an accident.

2. Belladonna: The Lady of Situations
I began to have love affairs after we'd been married five years. I had no excuse. I made one up about his not being interested in sex. He was never not interested in sex. The boy was my best friend's twin. It was crazy. I had babies! I stayed married seven more years. When I asked my husband "how could you put up with me?" He answered, "I thought you'd outgrow it."

3. The Man with Three Staves
He beat me with all three of them: fist, arm, foot. Some days I even believed he should. I hit back. We took a trip to Europe, he and I and his mistress. She wasn't much in bed and she whined all the way up the Zugspitze and on the Adriatic shore. We lied about all of it. I should have let her have him.

4. The Wheel
There was cocaine in master blasters, on trays, end tables, kitchen counters, bookcases. There were weekends, Friday to Sunday at that couple's house. I thought I was clairvoyant. I thought I could channel the dead. I thought I was a queen as months rolled by and I woke every morning with a nosebleed.

5. The One-Eyed Merchant
This minute is dust, and from minute to minute, dust and white. I carried it anyway. I didn't see a solution.

6. The Hanged Man

That man began me in the future past disaster. He didn't come up in this reading. Redemption is another deck of cards.

Michelle Glans

LAMENTO DECIRTE

Florida sighed its big wind
and our tree fell,
broke the gate's iron teeth,
sent so much water into the attic
that we could stand
among damp sheets of paper.

Abuelita held us like a monstrance
to see the eye of Matthew.
We pointed to the graying sun
shadowed by the haze of the hurricane.
We picked up the blown marigolds,
planted their yellow into little red cups
and placed them near the windowsill.
We prayed the rosary
with our hands held together like sap.

I used to think
that fear was one-dimensional
but now I know it is dry lightning
and Cadillac hearses
and empty coffee mugs.

Do you remember
that pine tree and all its needless
we liked to pull apart?
You always got the wishes
and saved them for me.

Do you remember Abuelita's big eyes,
like manzanilla olives in *picadillo*,
stuck somewhere between
a rainstorm and a sun-shower,
her freckles like orange soda stains,

the sound of her last leaving: that soft,
never-ending jingle of bangles?

Michelle Glans

I Wonder How Big the Sun Is There

We sit on my balcony to watch
lightning break on the Venetian and
eat stolen mango.
I take off my glasses. The
streetlights are quiet.

After a while she turns to me:
> *prima, life is nothing but second chances if you
> count them right.*

Once I grow tall enough she
pulls a tree branch
so I can climb to pick red fruit,
and when I look down, she is laughing. This is
all I can remember.

I want to imagine the warmth of her leaving as the
kind that smells like citronella
and makes your fingers stick together, a
spring rain or gardenias
flattened on pavement.

I want to say
*las luces de la calle
se hablan en un centelleo.*

I want to say
this is where she went there is
where she is going

I want
to bring mango sliced on
blue china

a spoon and dried sap gardenias
in the hallway one more phone
call
an opening in the sky
a word for this lump in my throat

Josh Mahler

Relief Following a Nightmare

What he said in secret about moonlight and regret,
I won't claim he was a god. Let it be an October day
when I linger on each syllable, passing into a bright

glare as I face what I've read about in the old books,
the details like evidence, the questions. We survive
behind doors left ajar, the mathematics of our bodies,

memory of skin. We stare at walls in stoic patience,
writing and listening, hoping and yearning for what
is preferred, yet never shared. Weakness is wanting

to escape from death. We conspire with the shadows,
submitting to a false blindness, the echoes we hear
as confusion, hangnails that are comforting because

they hurt, and truly so. In the quiet house, he looks
out the second story window. Down the driveway
to the fence, he crosses his arms under an ashen sky,

bare feet dirty from newly cut grass. I know this man.
He takes off his glasses, cleans them with his shirt,
and returns to where she moves from room to room,

preparing the scene. Who is she? What is her name?
With every kiss goodbye, another kiss begins. I close
the book, and they appear like how a finger feels after

being pricked by a thorn, hand holding a music box
from last year's anniversary, chimeless. I trace the hint
of a scar on my finger and remember the furniture

covered in dust. I don't fear the approaching storm.
I trust the trees, even as the leaves touch the ground.
Wander away, I tell myself, let your eyes fill with rain.

Michelle Bonczek Evory

BENEATH THE SURFACE

in cold caves no one sees
men of coal feed

soft apples to foals
who pull carts of black
lumps toward holes of light

the foals grow bigger than the holes
and become the earth they will never
leave the coal makes everything

it touches black and the men
make each other sandwiches
on Wonder bread

in the darkness they let fly
canaries who sing to the mares
songs of sunshine, and bloom

Michael J. Galko

ELEGY FOR A TREASURE DIVER, 1715

It was not work for Europeans, this diving–
holding one's breath for minutes at a time,
scratching one's hands on the sand or the hulk,

hoping for the few coins, the chest, a candelabra.
A slave doesn't ever know what ship it is, below.
The Spanish treasure fleet sank, taking the bounty

from the Philippines, from Peru, from Darien
and Mexico and the Spanish main. They wrecked
on this Florida coast. But who cares where it is.

The work is the same. Inhale. Dive. Scour the
wreck. Take another breath in the bell. Repeat,
repeat, repeat. Each time he rose, as they patted

his loin cloth for hidden coins, he could see some
of his fellow divers laid on the floating dock, gasping,
their veins bubbling, never to rise again. He could

feel his own lungs giving out, his limbs weakening,
eyes failing. These strange white men who dive not
for food, while they starve on the barren beach.

On his tenth dive of the third day it was him.
He simply couldn't hold it any longer. He saw his
mother, long since killed, his brothers, long since

dispersed, the layout of the small village that was,
once, home. He didn't swallow any seawater;
he was too good for that. They took the cup from

his right hand (Potosi silver) and the jade (Manila)
from his left. They carried him over to the others.

His last breath joined the infinite sky. The overseer

ordered the bodies burned away from the edge
of the salvage camp. He asked his deputy to bring
more divers from wherever he could find them.

And that was all for him. Still down there—chests
and bursting chests of treasure. The distant king
wanted it all, all the riches hidden by his cruel God.

Mary Buchinger

[FROM THE BOOK OF MINUTES]

⁓

Desire's trembling hand
lifts its apron
   dissects its dinner
      wipes the table
      beats the rug

⁓   ⁓

O lily stem of Desire
how you stand up the flesh
   flower the sleepless body

⁓

      (when Desire comes
my Nobody dies)

⁓

Desire trapped
      rattles its cage
   claws extending

   soft belly
      bare to sky

tail sweeps
      the wires

whips the
     walls it
calls and

    calls

~

Path to Everything
   Everywhere
      Desire says slipping
        underground

~

Desire sweeps in
 on two wings

 alights on the lip
of the feeder

  skirts the shells
emptied by others

  secures its oily seed
     its tender meat
  jet fuel

  Desire aloft
darts away

Rebecca Thrush

DEAR SIR/MADAM

I still get emails meant for you
                    RE: Alumni Newsletter
                    Hollywood's Golden Age, Free Gift Offer!
I'm not sure how we got so tangled
Same initials, different names
People used to tell me we looked alike too
As if these red and round cheeks were enough
To blend our faces into a singular smile

You could always bite into any crowd
And pull back with laughter, applause
My peppered kisses have always needed to be
Even more calculated than your mounting tabs
Filled with bubbling cups and smoke rings

But now as your cinder and musk fades
These misplaced messages are slowly going
Straight into my junk mail
As if the universe knows I'm starting to forget
How you took your coffee

So when I open your messages it makes me wonder
If maybe I could be as bold as your tropical prints
Or as soft as your weathered cottons
And as irrelevant as every offer is
I can't bring myself to unsubscribe
When it's all I have left keeping me tethered
To being a little more like you

Mark Smith-Soto

"COME AGAIN?"

"Always happy when I can" Helene quips
with a wink, a quick eyelid flick behind
thick, nose-pinching glasses, her big hips
adding a humorous twitch. It's a sign

of my innocence that I don't get it,
and she laughs at me, no, not with malice,
but with a little sigh, saying "Forget it
gay boy, didn't mean to give you *pause*,"

scratching at the air with a play growl.
Again, it takes me a second to catch
and reward the joke with the required groan,

mind snagged, surprised by the sudden fact
that I have just been winged by lust, and how
I want to get to the bottom of those puns.

Ciara Shuttleworth

TRINITY PRAYER

Father, I see your ruddy smolder
on the horizon. It has taken decades
to reenter your church
with curiosity instead of fear.

In a trinity of impossible, our family myths
are not important. Father,
the name of the son I'll never have
is Michael Ciaran, red-haired
hellion I call Beast in dreams. The holy ghosts,
Father, are impossible to grasp:
forget embrace. What is holy

lifts, always beaked: crows roadside, hawks
midflight, hummingbirds' orgasmic wing-shutter
and beak-thrust mid-feast. I feel chill and heat
off wings that flit near but never land. I am rarely able
to harness my own rage, bravado-
fueled, so like yours: incinerate
or raze what will not adore.

In a trinity of impossible,
your violence is instead prayer, a communion
to seek, and daughter is not caged at one angle
asking if any child birthed will have storms coiled
and writhing like chimera in their DNA.

There are the churches I entered
without you, sanctuaries and rituals I sought
to replace the religion of family mythology. The cherry
of a cigarette, a sun inhaled an inch risen
above the horizon. Breath halting to steady the same
after sex or nightmare. The trinity of alcohol,
nicotine, and pills I am no longer young

enough to hazard. Yes the only response
to any risk. Did I hope
to relinquish all control? I changed
my mind. Or I started walking.

But here I am, trying to kneel
with you. In a trinity of impossible,
Father, I am able to lie with my head
on your chest, your voice melodic and
soothing, the sun warming us through
broken windows we've together mended
to stained glass, to beauty, windows
we leave open wide to allow the
ghosts in, finally, to rest.

John Repp

PROSE ODE TO THE BLACK COLT

The bright morning after the latest blizzard, in the midst of our Sunday lope through the newspapers, a black colt materialized in the front yard—cropped tail, icicles encrusted on mane, nose & around both eyes—then lurched hock-deep to stand nodding between porch rail & propane tanks. He snorted the forsythia canes, bursts of snow glittering as they floated down. He looked in the window as Kathy fought to stay still. He turned & plowed down the shallow slope to the road, trackless, sparkling & palest blue till the colt—after flicking his tail & letting go a half-dozen steaming turds—whinnied, tossed his head & began picking his way north.

John A. Nieves

TRITINA B/W HALF-ELEGY (7" SERIES #2)

The hard red quiet, what took the place of space
of breath and song and secrets, this is the long
silence. And I do not wish I could say something

to you now. I wish only to hand you some thing
you would have handed me: a gritty cookie, the space
between forearm and bicep, a verse you could long

for. But this is not the remnant of a late-night sing-along.
This mute button can not be repushed, be made something
undoable. You were filled until you were empty—the space-

less space I can no longer reach for, something dark in my vowels

Jeff Hardin

A FOSTERING

At the home I lived in, floods arrived.
The woods turned swampy. I didn't
want to know where train tracks went,
submerged but visible beneath still-rising
waters. I was not yet burdened by memory.
I did not think about nations toppling,
forest degradation, coarsening speech
in the public sphere, growing animosities,
or the embrace of fictions more alluring
than faith or friendship. No revolution
had begun or ended. Church steeples
were not yet symbols of decay. Time
whispered its introductions. I searched
distances from which no train emerged.
Someone's hand held me back so that
I would not move closer, be swept away,
and the flood, the flood, has not relented.

Renee Gilmore

YOUR HANDS

Your hands hold the rosary in that way
that is yours, your mother's, her mother's,
back from the sod, the turf, how it was

taught. The beads on their delicate silver
chain, slide and bump over your papery
fingers so soft and worn like a cotton
quilt that has been washed of its sins over

generations. The beads, black, cool and
smooth, comfort as you slide through the
introduction, the decades, the conclusion—
59 chances for salvation. You mouth the
prayers with eighty years of certainty, and

keep the darkness at bay. You know the
flame grows short: the birds have made
their noisy migration, and the sun falls out
of the sky by late afternoon. You sit in your
flowered chair by the window, unperturbed
by what is to come: watching, waiting.

Matt Dennison

BOBBY EVANS

I remembered your name, the surprise
on your face at the nearness of our
ages as you sat in my study, rubbing
your cheek, gazing with your
one good eye (the other floating
in its basin of lid and pearl)
and the ease with which I offered
the fruits of my rented land after
hearing your knock on my door
that early fall evening, my near envy
of the simplicity of your gathering needs.
But I also remember my fear that you
would return, having been inside my house,
surveying, counting, touching my common objects
—for more than cigarettes, the first of which, requested,
the second called forth by two stiff fingers—for more
than pecans to gather and sell, forty cents a pound.
I remembered your name, Bobby Evans.
I made sure of that. As surely now
I question my own.

Lana Spendl

BURIED MEMORY

At dinner she ate far too much and before bed drank water too fast that pain cut through her chest and insides. Clutching the arm of the couch, she lowered herself onto the cushions. She wished she could throw up, but she had never been able to force it. She hobbled to bed, and in the middle of the night, woke up like a blowfish that had puffed itself too fast. She dialed the ambulance and—not wanting them to break the door down, nor tread dirty shoes in the house—she stepped outside, locked up, and laid herself onto the lawn with hair spread like a fan.

Up above, the stars glowed frost, and she wondered if the sickness—like Vaseline over camera lens—had exposed their beauty ethereal. Around her, streetlights mirrored sky—crowns bursting through trees yellow and red—and she ached with the sorrow from some ancient life that she had only found this night-magic now.

Gaylord Brewer

COURAGE

My old dog hesitates
at the tiles' edge, crossed easily
for a decade, now slippery menace
to her frail bones. How long
I mocked the notion
that courage was facing one's fears,
rather than the dull ignorance
of the intrepid.
What a fool. Come, little one,
brave beauty, fragile porcelain,
place one paw carefully
onto my arm, then the other
at your pace. Allow me the privilege
to lift you, carry you across.

Diane Scholl

NEWS OF THE WEEK

Sunday afternoons he read *The Times*
and listened to opera from a haze
of cigarette smoke, the sherry
for his heart. Daylight dwindling
to a thin gray scrim, we all gathered
in the cramped living room to watch
Meet the Press, he and my dad
arguing at the 16 black and white
inches of last week's news,
once interrupted by Batista's fall,
another time the revolt in Hungary.

It's how we learned about politics,
justice, love. When he spoke,
the words in his second tongue
came carefully, each one savored,
weighted, more than a little sad.

Mondays he'd head into another
week at the garage in the old Model A
he kept in tune, Cold War simmering
in its turbulent pot, arms race
driving us stealthily toward oblivion.

At the corner school kids hitched on
to the running board for a lark.
After all, there was so little to regret,
gears shifting, motor's steady chug,
the world in constant motion.

Marianne Kunkel

THE CARPOOL YEAR

After Walter Rane's painting *They Did Treat Me with Much Harshness*

*My wife with her tears and prayers, and also my children, did not soften
the hearts of my brethren that they would loose me.*
        —1 Nephi 18:19, *The Book of Mormon*

Kind Obispo, our neighbor
in Mérida, Yucatan, didn't buy a leather couch
for a four-year-old to angrily flop on, yet there I was
each weekday morning, splayed on cushions
and crying so loudly I drowned out my mother's *Gracias*.
Obispo's daughter was my age; at our Mormon church
I'd admire her crisp-white tunic dress embroidered
with bright poppies bigger than my face. It made sense
to ride together to preschool, despite
my family just arriving from Nashville
and me not knowing any Spanish. *They talk in words
I can't think about*, I pleaded with my mother,
her hand on my back both love and a shove
prodding me next door. In an old photo, I'm the child
squatting on pavement, arms crossed,
as my classmates sing and march around me.
My hot tears on the cool, mahogany leather
didn't stop; I was still sobbing in October,
the end of the rainy season. Tears couldn't stop
my mother from latching Obispo's screen door behind her
to putter home just as, years later,
they wouldn't stop a mango-size scar on my knee
after a car crash, my first boyfriend sexting
other girls, my parents' eventual divorce.
If not for a tube of artistic posters Mormon headquarters
mailed our Mérida chapel, I'd have wailed
in the children's Sunday School too
but I understood paint: a woman

draped around a man's hips, his wrists
tied behind him to a ship's mast. As men with whips
lunge at him, a smirking man steers the ship
through gray, spitting waves. I guessed this story
got worse—maybe the storm is God warning
the men to let up—and in the woman's
weepy face I recognized someone done crying for help
but not done crying, someone skilled in the art
of expressing pain, hopelessness
not a reason for silence
but its own worthy refrain.

Melissa Madenski

GRIEF VILLANELLE

I skip a flat stone
from the dock on the estuary bay
holding your ashes, a bit of bone.

Seals slice the water. Alone
I watch the morning make its way.
I skip a flat stone.

In the grass, a rotting spruce cone,
at my back spring winds sway
holding your ashes, a bit of bone.

Evergreens howl, a keening tone.
River pebbles roll away.
I skip a flat stone.

Near the dunes, reeds and loam
settle, shifting day by day
holding your ashes, a bit of bone.

Listen to the cormorant's moan.
I want to go; I want to stay.
I skip a flat stone
holding your ashes, a bit of bone.

Jeremy Paden

On Light

Years ago Mary Ruefle told a friend that one should stick one's tongue out and lap up the sun for fifteen seconds a day, that it's better than supplements; so every time I'm in the sun now, no matter how cold, and even in the rain and snow, in the fog and moonlight, I close my eyes, lean back my head, open my mouth, and stick out my tongue until my laughing stops me. The sllllness of a man in his late forties walking through the world with eyes closed, mouth open, tongue out, drinking in the sun, the rain, the moonlight, for no other reason than delight, for no other reason than how this connects him to the light. At times, I think of how the *g* and the *h* were slipped into the word *delite* to make it more like light and flight. At times, I think of Ian Charleson and Nigel Havers in *Chariots of Fire*, how gloriously they ran, mouth open, tongue out, gulping in the salty air of the beach—grown men, light-footed, delighted in their bodies as they moved through this world. How beautiful Ian was, even if briefly so. So beautiful, my mother loved him, not for his sandy brown hair, not for his eyes, blue like those of my father, but beautiful his spirit, beautiful how he ran with untrained abandon in his twill pants through the hills of Scotland and in his white cotton shorts along the beach, beautiful how he read before the congregation of the gathered from Isaiah, oh how the youths shall faint and even the young shall fall, loved him until the scandalous news of his death from AIDS. How slight his body would've been by the end. But wasn't he a good egg? Even as the darkness closed in around him, he chose to run, head back, mouth open, tongue lighting out.

Rosanne Osborne

MANEUVERS

The children drew bombs on the margins
        of their Big Chief tablets,
embossed their second-grade cursive
        with biplanes and jeeps.
Tracks of tanks rolled over the words
        of blameless primers.

They planted their victory gardens
        with the innocence of the poppies
of Flanders fields, and dug fox holes
        in their back yards to protect
puppies and kittens from the Germans
        suspected to live one block over.

War was remote, a star peeping from lace
        curtaining a darkened window.
Distance created a romantic haze
        that not even Nagasaki's cloud
penetrated as voices pledged the flag
        and sang of star-spangled reality.

Robert Eric Shoemaker

MAND
ORL
A GLORY

Tiresias
waited
a long time
for Iris to show.

The mountain top
is the metaphor, after all:
a penis
an inversion.
The interface of land and sky
has always been an ironic gate.

She remembered
that, a long, long time ago,
she had made a pact. Iris would show Tiresias
the world
and in exchange
Tiresias would tell Iris's fortune.

The fortune teller told Tiresias
of Iris and her secret.
The fortune came and went.

Tiresias blurted into the universe
and waited for the answer.

It finally came
in a blaze
and flash
of queer, blesséd light:

(As Iris floats above, an invitation of color,
Tiresias takes Iris's hand,
rips through the atmosphere,
and orbits.)

Planet – System – (song) – Planet – System
Tiresias approaches a planetary body
Tiresias approaches a meteor hurled from outer space
Tiresias approaches, a meteor hurled from outer space and is
caught
as in a trap as in a panic as in
a curly lick of fire brushing her armpit like don't even go there
don't even touch me, Planet

    See the vastness of the solar system   PROPHESY!
    First, praising sunlight, I sing sun,
    bringer of the day and banisher of the night, ☉,
    Sun, spitting one,
    charioteer your team your team   system, system

    Humans you have brought to this day you bring this day
    the heat, sun, the heat, day,
    you power sight! all that is right! who are we who are we
    to judge your mighty rays' proximity, we   systems of systems
                            we approach, a meteor hurled

                            let's do this one again:

    Humans bring you Sun to this day O Sun the banisher of night
    Humans bring you in to power sight
    Humans Humans cannot see
    We judge your mighty rays' proximity
    We, the cleansed, we the licked,
    You, piercer of the troposphere,
    Primal Beginner, Alpha Aleph
    Ariel atomizing your flame the blame the reaching lick
    comet lick asteroid shear our eyes our shame our pain pain your rays all praise

SEE THE VASTNESS OF THE SOLAR SYSTEM
        , Iris declares
SEE WHAT YE HATH WROUGHT

Tiresias tugs on the end of her rope on Iris's hand like a plastic bag
caught in the cartwheel,
squeaking,
squeaking,
Systems of Planets pinwheeling
and lost.

I've already had enough,
you think
she thinks
we all think
    system the system
it's not done with us yet
we've only just begun

bright bright burning message in your flight
turn like diamonds to your sight
glister my
glister my
blister flame and pole frost

   you are the lodestar you touch the secret Alchemical Light-Footed Messenger Burning
Thrice-Blessed Mercury
        ☉
        ☿

   let the flame and frost subdue me
Balancer give me Brother Balance
sainted Brother sainted Sister
sit a Buddha down upon my chest   let me breathe, let me breathe
                                        this hot flesh is just too liquid
regret undone like so many birds untethered
make me into your image:

Quicksilver
Quicksilver   just enough, I want just enough
                          I want to be able to breathe
                          I want to go into the spot
                          of my dreams
                          the space
                          where I orbit always
                          and fill space and take up my dreams in a hug
                          I want to be corporeal, please,
                          I pray corporeality
                          I pray
            NO MORE BLACK HOLES NO MORE BLACK HOLES
ANNNNNND....STOP!

Tiresias recalls
as she hovers a time in the heat
a mosquito sucking up blood
she recalls that moment
after the penetration has ended
after the small sob of it coming out
she hovers in the space before he pats her shoulder
then squeezes it
and that's where it is
that's the lingering doubt
the question:

"How much fun was that?"

And then he leaves and then every nerve is on fire and then she doesn't cry for 8 years.

Just dark space.

Do you know how meaningless you are in those moments?
Like an ant at the bottom of the sea
you are a paradox
which never existed
except in your mind, right now,
a flicker of existence
a mere possibility

he squeezes your shoulder
and you are a mechanism
of dark space

Make me the lodestar
open the secret
the secret mercurial quicksilver
adaptable
and fluid

blanket me, messenger
send me to a rest or a quick death

The planet flies through a sea of nothing
one side burning one side screaming in the freezing cold-cold quiet

—from Robert Eric Shoemaker's unpublished serial poem, *A Planetary Spell*

Marcia L. Hurlow

LOST ON CALLISTO

Let's say I decide to fly to the moon.
You're sure I'm headed to buy some fruit,
I'll be back home by the end of the week.

But what if I overshoot? I'm terrible
with directions. Maybe I'll land on one
of Jupiter's moons instead. How would you

find me? Don't shake your head, sigh, "She'll
figure it out." You would howl to Venus
for me. Say I telegraph that I'm cold

and everything is blue except the small
creatures turning backflips, tossing circles
of ice around my helmet like a game.

Would you know where to fly your spaceship
to return me to our home? I'm so far
from the grocery with the best produce.

Eight more groceries on this suburban
moon, its huge planet a food desert.
I circle again, ice up to my eyes.

Chelsie Taylor

UNSEASONABLE

On the fourth day of Christmas
the garlic sprouted from its bed.
"Unseasonable" I told the baby.
It's his first winter, and it's shown him more lightning than snowflakes.

I can't
trust the warm wind
that blows across our ears
so soon after the solstice.

Last year's Christmas morning,
we woke
to a light blanket of snow.
This year, I wore shorts
and our furnace held silent for three days after.

Joseph Anthony

PORCH STARLINGS

Starlings keep shortcutting
through the porch passage,
as I sit in the fall sun two feet or so below them.
I'm no threat.
No cat.
How they used to dive-bomb Calico.
How she deserved it.
Decimator of birds!

My peeling statue of St. Francis
shares the portico,
holding his cross and crossing his heart.
Pledging to nature, I guess.
He pulls his stone robes up daintily so we can
peek the carved sparrows clustering about his toes.
My lingering Catholic-Paganism.
I give his bald pate a pat.

I had a bad night.
I thought of my book that nobody wants.
I thought of my oldest child who seems
to want nobody.
My broken tooth, which I have benignly
ignored for two years,
decided to ache.

Some days, as little Alexander put it, are like that.

It's almost disrespectful the way the starlings
flit above me, as if I were
one more stone St. Francis.
The global warming sun peels me into a daze.
Almost November, I shouldn't be able to sit so stilly,
to feel as if I could recap all my lost slumber

from all my lost nights.
I gently press down on my sore tooth.
Perversity.
How sometimes it even feels good
to hurt.

Luke Wallin

NATIVE SPORTSMAN

In days gone by the Mississippi-born could put down a thousand dollars
for a lifetime hunting license. A ghost from the Chickasaw Tribe said

"Who you calling Native?" A buck in the Tombigbee Bottom said
"Who you calling Sportsman?" The ghost asked, "Are you familiar with

the concept of Animal Persons?" A woman from the Eco-League said
"I am," but men pointed to a sign: "NO WOMEN."

A couple of hunters showed their cards at the gate and were admitted.
Down in the field a fire was licking up dawn. Dogs in pickup cages

shivered while barking. A tractor pulling a flat-bed trailer loaded with
would-be killers armed with guns and whiskey and sandwiches

slowly made its hard-frost-way distributing each upon his stand.
After while the dogs, horses, and drivers ranged upon the swamp to

flush out deer. When a buck ran past a stand a Native Sportsman
fired his shotgun, shouted "Lifetime!" and the deer ran faster because

buckshot didn't kill right away but stung in Whitetail skin.
The wounded met in Canebrake Thicket to discuss "Whose lifetime?"

The ghost showed up and the chorus sang "Animal Persons have
issued you no invitation."

"I am caught betwixt and between!" the ghost declared.
"Quietly shoo," said one old buck, "as ghosts should do."

Young bucks with jejune antlers roared, "Gouge them while we can!"
Old bucks had been shot before and urged a campaign focused on the hounds.

The eco-woman-warrior said, "Times will be a-changin'."
"Not soon enough," one angry stag allowed, with blood dripping

down his leg. It was 1955, a bleakness time. The dying bucks decided
to surround just one of the Native Sportsmen for some end-times

conversation. They asked him for his precious card and trembling he
pulled it out to show. "You paid one thousand dollars for this?"
He nodded his head on his chinney-chin-chins. They circled and rammed him,
horns to horns, and when his groans had vanished on white-breath air

the deer declared "Uh huh." Then, from exertion and blood loss, they lay and died.
Law enforcement blamed the drivers who went into underground running.

Dogs continued to be bred by Native Sportsmen for their leisure. Eco-Woman
and the ghost trekked on. She held the lantern as he whined, "Too bright."

Luke Wallin

CYPRESSES IN DREAMS

Out on the water, boy after school, you fished alone into sunset.
Silence and bubbles, swirl of a gar, ancient things living around you.

Smell the fresh cypress, artesian well, lake swollen by the old river.
Blue heron flying, touching cool surface, extending her feet, sliding down.

Come back good father, picking me up, end of a long sawmill day.
Oh come back Mother, once out there fishing, rain lightning chased us away.

Stringer of shell crackers, strawberry bream, silvery glistening white perch.
Guard from the turtles, long water snakes, pull 'em up dancing and flashing.

Lonesome remember how empty you felt.
How god was so present so absent?

Paddle toward shore through the dusk of mosquitoes.
Remember the owls hooting loud on that water.

V. Joshua Adams

PSYCHE

from *psuchē*,
breath, or soul.
Soul in mind—
I learned this twice.
Once in a lecture
where the professor
sidled up
to the slim column
and tried to hide
as he talked
about unrequited love.
Then, watching my daughter,
as milk spilled
over honed granite,
her body going stiff and silent,
and hearing again
my voice bayonet the air
between her mother and me
while she lay,
a soundless surface
in the carriage.

Denise Duhamel

WHACKADOODLE

Almost a year after my mother's death,
on July 7, 2022, the word "wackadoodle"
makes its first appearance in *The New York Times*.
My mother was a fan of the word,
often peppering her sentences with it.
She visited me in Florida the day after
Trump won in 2016. When I'd sent her a ticket,
I thought we'd both be celebrating
the first woman president. When I picked her up
at the Fort Lauderdale airport, nothing
looked different. I was baffled, sure
that the planes of the world would stop flying,
their wings too heavy with grief.
I know, of course, planes don't have feelings—
and I was projecting onto those silver beasts.
My mother and I tried to talk about
other things, but we kept coming back
to America's withering future. Once in a while
my mother would say, *We just have to
give him a chance, I guess.* And I would nod
though deep inside I knew Trump was a flimflam
sham, that things would get worse.
We didn't know yet that that this would be
my mother's last visit, that soon Hurricane Irma
would destroy my apartment. We didn't know
she would wind up in a nursing home ravaged
by Covid. We didn't know the U.S. would be ravaged
by an insurrection. She was ravishing
that November and men kept trying to talk to her,
no hint of death anywhere in her torso.
One old dude wearing a Scarlet's Strip Club cap
cornered her while I was in a restaurant
bathroom. *All flirting is ruined*, my mother said.

All I can think of is that whackadoodle
grabbing women by the you-know-what.

Pat Owen

I TRY TO REMEMBER HER A TODDLER

standing in front of the fridge
watermelon juice streaked down
her chest. She was all mine,
recently part of my body.
I could sweep her up, face
to face, kisses all over her head.
You are my sweet baby I'd chant,
putting her in a basket on my bike,
peddling around the neighborhood
describing all we were seeing.

Now I go to her for advice, she
solid and professional in her
long white lab coat, a responsible
mother with adult daughters
of her own.

I try to bring back holding her close
in a waiting room
her small body hot, fast-beating heart,
temple wet against my own,
stroking her head, tender
and soft as a melon. Every ounce
of my will lasered to keeping
her alive. Our survival interlocked.

Donald Illich

EPIDERMIS

When we wake up,
someone has removed our clothes,
leaving nothing in closets or drawers to adorn ourselves.

We guess this is supposed to teach us a lesson, but it doesn't.

We shield privates
as we search for clotheslines
still gripping shirts and pants.

No luck, even towels are burning in pyres.
We feel embarrassment that resists leaving.

Soon, though, we need coffee (drink carefully)
to go to work. We start by averting eyes

from special places, but soon a Tootsie roll joke
moves us forward, we learn to take care of each other's bodies,

notice blemishes that might be skin cancer,
formulate remedies for horrible rashes.
Soon we love one another more strongly,

because we can see how vulnerable we are,
an epidermis covering flesh that can be poked and skewered,

all of us alike in our weaknesses,
nothing between us and the world.

Hollie Dugas

WHEN GIRLS BECOME BIRDS

It begins with the nature of
my full nude body ordained
art, painted awkwardly within
the cathedrals of fragile eggs,
the bitter taste of insects
budding in my throat,
and the dream of gaining
wind—to, one day, waking
with thick plumage vital
for flight. I am nobody
if not a good little dodger.
Look, here comes another
man on a motorcycle.
I do not flinch at death and
blood and splattering
my chest on glass anymore.
This world is nothing
to quail about. I've preened
the hefty specks of damsel
stuck to my velvet wings and
let them fall like small creepy
mites from my feathers
to dirt. I am no longer
mistaken as a dainty
hourglass-shadow shifting
under clouds. I'm learning
the sweet tuneful language
of my kind, renouncing
all of life can be held
in a tiny straw basket. Agile
and untamed, life is a ballad
of color, blooming
within me like wildflowers.
I've taken to the tops

of buildings like a holy beast,
the gift of starlight nesting
in my softened bones.

James B. Nicola

EVOLUTION

When an ape
washed a grape
they thought he was drinking

or deranged.

Then an ape
peeled a grape
and everyone's thinking

changed.

Nonfiction

Chris Reitz

Essay on Cover Art: *Turbulence* by Ying Kit Chan

Ying Kit Chan is perhaps best known for his works on paper; his dark, calligraphic lines that evoke both Chinese calligraphy and industrial and mining landscapes, common in West Virginia and Kentucky, where he draws much of his inspiration. But the artwork that adorns this issue's cover departs from these earlier projects. It depicts natural repercussions: a tornadic cyclone, burned out trees. Climate's response to human influence perhaps. Or maybe better, a tension—a battle, even—between human and natural forces.

This painting, alongside more colorful compositions on view at a recent exhibition at Moremen Gallery, signals a return to painting, a medium he mastered as a student and young artist. To hear him tell it, these paintings came about through a natural evolution in thought about the climate crisis. Once upon a time, Chan's art captured and reflected on the state of environmental degradation. This older work explored the aesthetics of industrial production and devastation. That exploration soon evolved into what Chan calls "Geo-Ethics," artwork that concerns humanity's relationship with the natural world and the possibilities for ethical or at least sustainable living therein. Today, his thinking focuses as much on the people and politics of climate change as it does on the material fact of climate disaster. Although each of the paintings in this recent series has a natural referent (nuclear waste at Bikini Atoll is a recurring theme, as are wildfires), his thoughts are occupied by the human forces that prevent climate action, and the fundamentally different worldviews humans maintain about the natural world (about global warming, about microplastics, even about who and what the natural world is for).

To better understand how these paintings *reflect* this political tension even if they do not *depict* it, we must turn to Chan's painterly education and his return to painting in this new work. Throughout the American Midwest in the 1970s, academic art training focused on formal compositional techniques, many of which made use of Hans Hofmann's "push-pull" theory of composition. "Push-pull" refers to the use of alternating areas of gestural, abstract lines and geometric blocks of color to create the illusion of space and of tension in a painting. Many of Hofmann's students, who were trained in New York, moved to the Midwest to teach, and art schools in the region quickly adapted and adopted push-pull techniques into something of an abstraction lingua-franca. Even if you don't understand how it works, you've likely seen a painting that uses this compositional strategy. Which is why it is a helpful starting point for Chan's painting. He received his BFA from the University of Oklahoma and then his MFA from the University of Cincinnati. Both schools at the time (the early 1980s) were steeped in formalist practice. By adopting these formal devises for his "return" to painting—formal devises that rely on opposition and tension—Chan points to the tense ideological origins of our current climate crisis rather than its physical (industrial) origins.

Turbulence (2022), the artwork on the cover of this issue, takes up the formal color field composition strategies of Chan's midwestern roots, adapting them to the calamity of his ecological present. Like all "push-pull" compositions, the painting creates a sense of depth through juxtapositions of gestural brushstroke and smooth surface. However, where a more traditional composition would only feature the illusion of depth, Chan's painting is truly three-dimensional. The white, swirling structure on the surface of the painting reaches out into the space of the viewer. This object is not painterly but instead industrial plastic waste. The tension in the work is thus not just between formal elements but also between a more gestural, tornadic (and painterly) landscape and the swirling, literal refuse of industrial production. In this way, Chan uses familiar painting composition strategies to hold together depictions of the natural world and the real industrial material harming it. In turn, the artist doesn't just represent climate crisis in his art, he generates in his compositions the feeling of unresolved conflict that is the backdrop (or perhaps *origin*) of climate debates. In these compositions, painted surfaces seem to exist outside of, but also determined by, the industrial material glued to them. The materials are different not only in texture but in origin (Chan makes his paintings and finds his industrial material). It is this very irreconcilability that operates as the support for our fraught political debates too—debates that concern, but never really fix, the rapidly deteriorating natural world.

The Louisville Review

Dianne Aprile

KEEPING RECORDS

The last time we moved the old corrugated boxes, full of 78s, heaving and hauling them up and down stairs, scooting their dead weight across carpets and hardwood floors, it finally hit me.

Marriage is like my mother's old 78s.

Circular. Fragile. Heavy. Old-fashioned.

Lyrical. Scratchy. Sexy.

Laden with memories. Filled with the blues. All that jazz.

My mother bought her records in the '40s, before The War, before marriage and children, before suburbs and subdivisions and stereos entered her life. She bought them while employed at a music store in downtown Louisville, Kentucky. More precisely, and quite oddly, it was a store that sold records and men's ties and silk stockings. It was her livelihood as a single woman, dating my father, living with her parents, paying her way.

She liked selling records; she liked listening to them and meeting other people who shared her growing passion for jazz. She bought records the way her girlfriends bought high heels or Hershey bars. She couldn't get home fast enough to try them out, devour them.

The ones she liked most were the off-the-record records, music recorded by black musicians, not usually played in white establishments. "Race records" is what they called them in those days. The voices spinning off those shimmering discs spoke to her in a language she was inexorably drawn to: suffering and sorrow, love and loss, lust and injustice, and at the heart of it all, a full-throttle, fathomless faith. In the divine, perhaps but even stronger faith in the body and its power to wound and heal, like the music called jazz.

When she married, my mother quit working. My dad didn't like the idea of her holding a job, paying her way, making acquaintances he didn't know. Maybe she was tired of it, too, although I don't believe she was asked.

Still, she never tired of the music that had seduced her, so early, so fiercely. She played it throughout my growing up years. It was the soundtrack of my childhood.

When 33s replaced 78s, she bought a HiFi, a satiny cube of dark mahogany that opened like a jewelry box, whose turntable could accommodate the old heavyweights as well as vinyl 33s and the newer, smaller, lighter plastic 45s.

She played "Strange Fruit" and "St. Louis Blues" and told me about the juke box operators who leaned against the record-store counter, trying to pick her up, show her a good time. She talked about the music, the people who sang it, and how the singers of the era—who all sounded the same to me at the time—were each one distinct from the other. Scatters. Swingers. The great blues singers. She wanted me to love the music she loved.

But I liked other singers, simpler tunes. I wasn't ready for complexity. And then she died.

And no one wanted the records. Not my father. Not my brothers. Each caught up in his own private grief. I asked a friend to help me haul them out of my father's house to my apartment. My mother had stacked them precariously in boxes—some in hard covers, some in flimsy paper jackets, some as naked and vulnerable as I felt after she was gone. I can't remember much about the day we moved the records from her house to mine.

But I can tell you this: the most common wound to a 78 is the loss of a chunk of itself from its clean round edge. Like a bite from a cookie. Like a circle broken.

At my apartment, I kept my mother's records in a hallway closet and in my basement locker. They seemed heavier now that she was gone, more cumbersome, and yet holding them in my hands, touching the grooves that still bore her fingerprints, was, I knew, as close as I could come to grasping who she was.

When I was a child, I liked to open the doors of my mother's china cabinet, the one that housed the dishes she brought out only on special occasions. The ruby-red decanter, smooth glass etched in roses, and its six small matching cups. What clues did that long-necked carafe offer to my mother's hidden self. I opened those doors, just to stare inside, never to touch, never to hold, simply to witness. A kind of meditation.

The records were the same for me. But I handled them: so cool to the touch, that deep dark swirling center I couldn't fathom. The label with its mysterious musical icons.

A bluebird. A listening dog. I would look and touch but never play.

A few years after my mother died, I met the man I later married. He loved jazz, too. I learned that right away. I showed him my mother's 78s in the storage locker and in the closet. He shook his head at my hidden treasure. He drew one unblemished 78 from its brown wrapper, held it thoughtfully in his hand, let his index finger gently trace its smooth, curving circumference.

I sensed that he knew then that those records would be a part of every progression in the lifesong we would create together. I took it as a sign: he understood I could never part with them; he understood me.

But a year later, when we moved together to an ancient six-plex a mile or so away, he cursed the boxes and the 78s teetering inside them all the way up from the basement locker of my old place, out to the trunk of the car and up three flights of stairs to our new place. Less than two years later, as we packed for a move to our first house, he balked at the prospect of again hauling boxes of records we hadn't touched since the last time we moved them. Disheartened, I vowed I would move them myself. But he joined me, solemnly, in the silent ritual.

I was filled with relief each time the records made the journey safely to whatever space we were inhabiting.

Two years and a son later, we moved again. With minimal grumbling, the 78s were borne down from the attic to the car, then to the dark, dank basement of our blue bungalow.

Where they stayed, unplayed, until the next time they had to be moved.

My mother's records. They are his history now too. They are my past become his. They are like marriage, these spinning black holes of harmony, melody, crescendo and rest. These burdensome brittle artifacts of love, of family, of local history, of distant drumbeats, of connections to earth and animal, sorrow and sex, money and passion, jealousy and betrayal and time spinning spinning spinning.

Our last move in our hometown was to five wooded acres on a rocky ridge, above a winding country road—a house blessed with a ground-floor storage room. It was easy, this time, stowing my mother's records in a place of safe-keeping. Our son was old enough by then to help with the hauling, shouldering his share of the freight.

Before my mother left her record-store job, she saved enough money to buy bedroom furniture for her marriage to my father. They slept in her solid maple four-poster all their lives together. They hid their valuables and stored their secrets in the drawers of the tall bureau. They kept an eye on one another in the mirror above the dresser. When she died and my father started over again at marriage, I took the bed and bureau to my apartment for safekeeping. Later a brother divorced and found himself in need and took the bed for himself. Then my father divorced and asked to have it back from my brother who, by then, was himself remarried.

The bed had value. But no one wanted the records.

Outdated. Old-fashioned. Scratchy. Cumbersome. Laden with memories. Filled with blues.

I sit sometimes in the house where my marriage, in its latest habitat, now unfolds; a house whose windows open up, in waves, to extremes of darkness and light, thunderhead and moonshadow; a home that is forty years old, exactly the same age as my marriage. Not surprisingly, the sprawling frame tilts and slants and dips and—who knows—perhaps at night when we're sleeping, swirls and spins, trading licks with our dreams, improvising harmonies, mixing memory with melody.

Like my mother's records.

Like marriage.

Fiction

Patricia Foster

THAT LIFE

Even at noon the church smelled like beeswax and sweat. Within thirty minutes, the men's shirts were stained deep under the arms and the women's dresses clung tight to their thick upper bodies and hung in limp folds between their legs. It was early July, 1936. Sitting in a pew that first Sunday, Martha heard the grind of a truck's axle as it banged against the gravel road beyond the church, advancing and braking its way down the steep grade to the mines while outside the window, gnats whirled in dreamy clouds above the thorny bushes. And yet what thrilled her were the soft, exultant chords from the organ as if Mrs. Curtis, the organist, was secretly calling them together, connecting them, lulling their differences. Oh, to be called, to be chosen, to be a part of the believers! Martha leaned forward, closing her eyes and letting the music fill her until she heard everyone moving, getting up to sing, singing and swaying. Martha stood too but she held herself still. It was the stillness that scared her.

To calm herself, she looked around at the familiar faces: dry, sallow Mr. Wiebel, a widower, and the superintendent at the mine; his stair-step children; Mrs. Violet Ware, who had occasionally been seen wearing lipstick; Mrs. Ware's sulky husband Calvin. There were also the Qompts, a family so religious, so bold in the spirit that everyone feared their judgment; and Regina, her pretty friend from last year. Most important, of course, was the preacher, a dark-haired man who paced theatrically before the altar, his face at times radiant with hope and the blessings of the Lord and other times shadowed by grief and the lonely sadness of their worldly sins. As he paced, he told them how he'd once served a mission in Africa where he'd watched young women die in childbirth, their babies turned backwards and sideways, unable to be born.

"And like these blessed women in Africa," he said, turning to face them, "we too see things turn sideways and backwards inside us."

Though Martha listened attentively to his memories of Africa, what mesmerized her was the story of the boy in the woods. "Late in the evening," the preacher began, pausing in his trek from the pulpit to the organ, his voice softening as if he were talking intimately to each of them, "a young boy was sent to gather wood, loose branches he could cut down and stack for his family. He wasn't old enough or strong enough to cut big branches, but he could sort and carry the broken limbs to keep the stove going." He told them that on this day the boy wandered further than he usually did, climbing up small hills and pushing through brush, gathering and stacking until his sacks were full. But as he wandered through the woods, the sky was beginning to darken, surprising him, and when he came to a crossroads—the graveled road barely a path with many switchbacks—he heard the menacing screech of an owl and a rustling in the bushes. He saw dark clouds massing with barely a sliver of light. Scared suddenly of the approaching nightfall, and possibly a storm, he decided to take a shortcut.

"And why not?" The minister looked at each of them as if posing the question directly. "He was just a boy, hungry and tired. He wanted to have supper and wanted to see his mama smile at how much wood he'd carried. So, he hurried on. But what he didn't know was that he'd misjudged the crossroads. He'd walked further than he remembered and instead of the path leading him home, it led him deeper and deeper into the woods."

"And this," the preacher said, "*this right here* is the parable of our lives. Like that boy, we venture out to do what's necessary. We work and we labor to keep food on our table, to have a bed to sleep in, to help ourselves and each other, but some days, well, yes, some days we get tired. Some days we stray beyond our boundaries. Some days we get scared or confused. And this, my friends, is when we want relief. We want dry shoes and a fire. We want a plate of buttery potatoes and our radio program and we want familiar voices around us. And so, we take a short cut. We abandon the harder path, the one that will cost us—yes, it always does—though we know it will get us home."

He bowed his head as if he were reminiscing about his own life, his own crossroads, and when he looked up again his eyes were dark and shiny with feeling. His voice was so faint, so low they had to lean forward in their pews. "And it's this, brothers and sisters, this that we got to wrestle with, this urgent choice between the short cut and the hard path." There was a pause, a weighted silence. No one moved. No one dared sigh or cough. Everyone waited, feeling a restraint in their muscles and a quickness to their breath. And then, very quietly the preacher stretched out his arms to them, inviting them, beseeching them, "Come," he said, his voice once again deep and vibrant. "*Come.*" And when the music began, soft, soothing and then more urgent, it carried them, clothing them in the warmth of the altar where they knelt, bound together as one, determined to take the hard path, not only to choose it but also to relish in the choosing.

Martha watched, astounded as these worn and familiar people seemed to cast off the ordinary misery of their lives.

It wasn't until the third Sunday that Martha rose when the preacher's call came. That day she closed her eyes, moving as if pulled by a secret inner force though she knew it wasn't the feeling she was supposed to have. She didn't feel holy. She didn't feel drenched in the blood of the lamb. She didn't feel repentant or lost in the spirit or bound to the Holy Ghost. What she felt was less conspicuous kneeling with the believers than sitting with her two younger sisters in a pew and having Mrs. Qompt, who often sat behind her, stare at her with those dark, beady eyes as if she were heir to her family's sins. Her father drank. Her mother, tired and frazzled, did not come to church. By now, Martha knew that every Sunday Mrs. Qompt, standing tall and straight as she testified, reveled in deeds of earthly virtue and called out those who did not follow the law.

It was only after Martha knelt that day—feeling ordinary and uncertain and self-conscious—that Mrs. Qompt began to pay attention to her, to kneel beside her at the altar as if she were one of the chosen. The next Sunday, Mrs. Qompt sat beside Martha in the pew and casually pulled Martha's hair away from her face, her hands surprisingly soft, though the gesture was practical. When she handed Martha a bobby pin, Martha swelled with pride. Her own mother had never brushed her hair, had never taken notice of her except to pile on more responsibilities or to correct a task poorly done. Martha had never been special, but now with Mrs. Qompt sitting beside her she wondered if she too might choose the hard path. Briefly, she glanced over at Regina to see if she'd noticed, but Regina was staring out the window.

It wasn't until early fall, several months later, the trees shedding their leaves, the leaves blanketing the slag heaps and transforming them into shifting, rustling mountains of color, that everything changed. Now there was the smell of wet boots, of wood smoke. Kids raced heedlessly down the mountain roads, knowing that soon those roads would be slick with ice, trucks skidding, fathers shouting, night crews assembled. It was on a Sunday in October that Mrs. Qompt stood up in church as she always did. That day she looked austere but proper, her face composed, her dark eyes glittering as she scanned each of them, sparing none. Attentively, she smoothed her black skirt, making them wait as if it were her due. "The Lord forgive me," she began in a firm, level voice, "but there is among us, yes, among us a sinner against the Word, a fornicator who has soiled her vows." Martha sat up straighter, feeling a twitch of fear, a flutter in her chest. "The Lord forgive us all but right here, yes, here with us, there is a Jezebel who taints our place of worship." The worshipers went quiet, waiting. And then a nervous ripple raced through the pews, a mixture of anticipation and dread, an anxious flurry of excitement. To Martha's surprise, Mrs. Qompt turned and pointed a bony finger at her friend Regina. "I seen her... *that one*, crouching, all undone... on the road at night." Martha gasped, not only at this claim of transgression but at Regina's bowed head and humbled posture as if by her silence she was admitting the offense and accepting her forthcoming exile.

But Regina? How could that be? No, it was wrong. It had to be.

"*Jezebel!*" her sisters squealed as they rushed down the road after church, thrilled with the word that sounded both indecorous and happy. They kicked at the rocks, scattering them to the sides of the road, though they knew better than to scuff their shoes. "*Jez-e-bel! Jez-e-bel!*"

"Get lost." Martha barked. "Go on!" And the girls ran on ahead of her, still giggling.

No, it was stupid. Martha refused to believe what Mrs. Qompt had said, certain Mrs. Qompt was mistaken, had seen someone else on the road the night she'd gone for the doctor. Until this year, when Regina had moved on to the high school in West Jefferson, Martha and Regina had been pals, walking together to the local school, Regina older and more daring, but friendly and often silly as if accommodating Martha for being younger, less knowing. What Martha had most loved about those walks was that once out of sight of their mining company houses the two of them would sing rowdy songs, shouting at the top of their lungs. Their favorite, the one that made Martha feel giddy and grown-up, was "Way Up on Clinch Mountain," a song they belted out, ritually performing all the necessary gestures and antics. "*Way up on Clinch Mountain/I wander alone/I'm es drunk es the devil/Oh, let me alone!*" How thrilling that third line! Dramatically they stumbled and leered and pretend-puked before prancing and high-stepping like the devil, using their fingers as horns.

"*Way up on Clinch Mountain*," Martha murmured as she walked, but even whispering the words seemed a betrayal. How could Regina, barely fourteen, who favored a lilac-colored blouse with a bleach spot spattering one sleeve and snorted at the stupidity of boys, be doomed, exiled? Why, she'd be kept at home. It just couldn't be.

But it was. For the next month, Regina stayed at home, mostly out of sight, going neither to school nor church, though Martha saw her once on her porch with her mother wringing out clothes and once squatting in the side yard washing her dog in a tub of water, the soap suds bubbling in the air, Regina laughing as if nothing had happened until she looked up, saw Martha, and went immediately silent.

At home, Martha's sisters began to make up stories about Regina as if she were part of a grotesque fairytale, a princess shamed and outlawed, expelled from the kingdom but worthy of attention. They talked about "watching" her, trying to "catch" her doing something, anything that could titillate their curiosity. "I *saw* her outside her house," the younger one whispered, "making pee-pee and *not* in the outhouse. Right in the yard."

"Oh, please, shut up," Martha insisted, irritated and heartbroken. "You don't know anything."

"No, I saw her. It's you who don't know anything! And she used her *hand* to wipe herself!"

But then Annie Laurie, the middle sister started crying. "It's not true what they say, it's not true that the baby will have webbed feet and a pinched head. I think, I think—" she sniffled "that the baby's *magical*. I think that's what they're afraid of." And the very next day she collected rocks alongside the road, scrubbed and polished them with soft rags she stole from the kitchen until they were smooth and striated, almost pretty, rocks she used to make the outline a heart outside Regina's window.

Unlike her sisters, Martha said nothing. One day she hated Regina. The next, she blotted her out as if she could erase her. The next day she missed her, remembering not just the fun they'd had singing, but the silly plots they'd hatched, the way Regina had insisted they secretly help a good-looking boy named Ray Douglas.

"All the town girls are *mad* for him," Regina had explained a year ago as they'd dawdled, stopping to gossip, on their way home from school. "But he doesn't pay them any mind. He has to help his family."

Ray Douglas, Martha knew, was from a home like theirs, impoverished and provincial, not some town place with rose bushes and ivy, the father a manager, a mother in aprons. She'd seen him a few times at the Commissary, a lanky, big-shouldered boy, who played football for West Jefferson, with a shock of dark hair that splashed over his forehead and the palest skin she'd ever seen, almost translucent, blue veins at his temples. Martha knew it didn't matter one whit if the high school girls were madly in love with him because none of their families would let them have anything to do with him—beyond cheering for him on the football field—because of his dad. What happened had occurred years ago but everyone swore it was the godawful truth: when a wall of falling rock crushed Slim Whitney's leg in a side tunnel of the #7 mine, Jimmy Douglas, Ray's dad, had been practically right there, at least nearby, but instead of helping Slim or keeping him company until help came, Ray's dad managed to haul himself out of the tunnel and run home. No one really knew much more, only that after Slim Whitney lost his leg (and his job), Jimmy Douglas became a drunk, a mean drunk who sat on his porch on Saturday mornings, heckling anyone who walked by. "Hey fatso," he'd call out to Mrs. Hanson with her brood of children. "Got any more them brats coming outta that barn? Need you a milker?" Then, he'd cackle and burp and lift his jar, taking a deep, indignant swallow.

"He's lonely," Regina said, staring somberly down the road where Ray, just off the school bus, was walking home. "I mean, you can *see* it in his eyes."

Martha looked in the same direction but all she saw were stray cats prowling in the bushes, then leaping out and scratching in the dirt. "We could leave him notes," she said only to cheer up Regina. "I mean, in the bushes. You know, something to strike his funny bone and make him laugh."

To Martha's surprise, Regina was ecstatic. She clutched Martha's hand, calling her "the absolute smartest thing around."

Instantly committed, they tore out pieces of school paper, folded them in half to make them look prettier, used their best cursive to write his name, and then penciled messages inside: "*If you're lost, now you're found!*" "*Go two feet and pretend you vanished.*" "*Big Eyes Are Watching You!*" and "*If you're reading this, you're headed somewhere new.*"

Of course, Ray never let on that he got any of their messages though they feverishly kept adding new ones, tucking them between branches, under leaves, sometimes lodged beneath a single, craggy stone. Once they saw Ray passing by some of the raggedy bushes where they'd hidden several notes, edges of the paper flapping into view. "*Turn*," Regina whispered. "Turn and *look*." But he only jogged moodily past, his eyes on the ground.

The next day Martha secretly plucked one of the notes they'd left for him, and then, as if surprised it was gone, showed Regina the empty spot. "See," she said, but Regina looked at the spot with distraction. "He doesn't get it," she said.

Only then did Martha realize Regina wanted Ray to notice *her*. Martha felt outraged: the game was about *them*, not Ray. "Maybe he's too stupid to get it," she said defiantly.

Regina turned, eyes narrowed. "What do you know?" she asked, then walked on ahead, her long curly hair whipping out behind her in the raw wind.

"A lot," Martha murmured as she pulled the note out of her pocket and began tearing it up, almost viciously, pleased to see the confetti pieces, tiny and jagged, floating to the ground.

"*I see you, I see you*," Annie Laurie sing-songed, coming up behind her and nodding at the mess.

Martha swatted at her sister—"Why, you little spy!"—but then, as if she hadn't done enough, she kicked at the scraps of paper and watched them leap and flutter and then settle further down the road. "Stupid," she muttered.

But two days later, Regina, beaming, rushed up and grabbed Martha's hand, swinging it playfully as if they'd never had a spat and telling her in an excited gush about the new puppy her daddy had found up on Finch Road the night before and brought home, a puppy now asleep under her bed. "It's a ball of fur and a mouth," she laughed, giddy with the news as they walked towards the school. She squeezed Martha's hand. "And I can keep it."

Neither of them ever mentioned Ray Douglas again.

And yet now, barely a year later, Regina had not only abandoned their girlhood pranks, but had also betrayed everything about growing up that Martha longed for. Where was the romance, the independence, the shy but certain improvisation meant to carry them away from here to a different life? *Oh, let me alone!*

In late November, Martha was surprised to see Regina early one morning dawdling with her dog along the road by her house. It was a coal-black dog with one white patch circling the left eye and a fat, bushy tail. For a moment Martha crouched, hiding, her fingers touching the sharp rocks and bits of coal flung from the trucks as they shuddered down the grade. Her hand closed around a sharp stone, its edge biting into her palm. Furious at Regina for not appearing tragic, she rose quietly, stealthily, ready to throw. She took aim, her arm poised, her muscles taut, but when she saw how Regina's lilac-colored shirt was loose at the bottom, the hem a slightly darker color, let out to cover the bulge, she couldn't do it. Her arm went slack, and she was about to let the stone drop when, further away, on the opposite side of the road, she noticed a tall, steadfast figure in black, waiting. Waiting to see if she had the courage? Waiting to see if she was special? Regina had moved on, was closer to her house. Not once had she looked around as if she were oblivious to the drama. Now the most that Martha could do was toss the stone in her direction where it bounced off a mud pile and rolled under a bush. Stupid! And yet when Martha looked up, Mrs. Qompt nodded.

The next Sunday, the small, dark-haired preacher, who was, to Martha, as central a figure to the church as Mrs. Qompt, was replaced by an old man, thin and reedy, with a rough country voice he used to yell at them about hell, about their sins, their vanity, and their disobedience. He told no stories and allowed Mrs. Curtis to play the organ only at the beginning and end of the service. Mostly, he chastised and rebuked and tried to bring forth the Lord's holy wrath as if he meant to badger them to salvation. Mrs. Qompt, Martha noticed, listened as attentively as ever, but Martha, disappointed and confused—she didn't know these were circuit preachers—left immediately after the service, hurrying away from the cloistered group that always circled the preacher.

What had happened? Even the organ music had seemed morose.

"It's run off." Annie Laurie leapt from the porch when she saw Martha coming back from church. In the last month, the younger two girls had gotten bored with the church and quit going.

"Hush up." Martha was in no mood for Annie Laurie's nonsense.

"It's Regina's *dog*. It's lost. I saw her sitting on her front steps weeping. Her ma won't let her out of her sight."

"Serves her right." Martha pushed past her sister, her thoughts darkening. Regina had taken a short cut. That's what she'd done; she'd forfeited her right to everyone's compassion. She got what she deserved. As Martha moved quietly toward the bedroom she shared with her sisters, hoping to avoid her mother's ready list of chores, she wondered for the first time, why Regina had let go and gone to bad. If she'd done what Mrs. Qompt said she'd done, "soiled herself," then not only her soul but also her insides were all torn up and that lilac colored shirt was shielding an awful bloody mess.

All afternoon, Martha argued with her sisters, stole Annie Laurie's pie, cramming it into her mouth, and then dropped a pile of washed clothes in the dirt. Though she hurried to pick them up, her mother had seen from the kitchen window. "That's enough!" She stormed out and slapped Martha briskly across the face. A not unexpected punishment. But it was too much. Too soon.

Martha ran. She didn't care where. Anywhere. Just to be away. Away from duties and grumbling and cruelty. Away from confusion. She ran heedless of direction, but her path was familiar: she found her way to the church where she could sit on the back steps alone. No one would be there at this time. She flung herself onto the top step and stamped her feet, her mind a fury of resentment. She spit at the dirt, at the air, into the dead leaves. She hated them all! She stamped her feet again, but her tantrum was interrupted by a whimpering, puking noise, and from under the steps came the dog, its black coat slick with phlegmy-looking filth, leaves and twigs knotted in its tail. The eye nestled in the white patch, was half-closed from a running sore, yellow pus oozing from one corner. But when the dog saw Martha, it wagged its tail, became suddenly friendly, whimpering and nudging her leg with its nose. Instinctively, Martha began petting it, letting its wet nose nuzzle her hand—"oh, disgusting!" she murmured with affection as the dog's tongue licked her hand as if she were food. "Why, you're hungry, aren't you? You're just a poor little messed up thing." She was cooing, bending her head to the dog, hugging it, closing her eyes and stroking its head, which had no slime and only smelled slightly of vomit. She would protect it, take it back. She would—

"Git!" The whack of the stick so startled her she leapt up, the dog squirming with pain, then running away. Danny Qompt, the oldest

Qompt boy, probably sixteen, sneered at her, stick in hand. "Whadya think you're doing? That's *her* dog."

"She's hungry."

"So?"

"So, I could get her some food. She's just a dog."

"Not you." The way he said it shocked her, his stare reproving, unrelenting. No, it was more than that: his stare was menacing, as if now *she* was shameful, as if she would have to be dealt with. He came closer. At first, he just stared at her as if scrutinizing her face, then he grabbed her hand, twisting it hard, pinching, and pressed it to his trousers, his grip firm, his eyes like flints. He teased the stick against her legs as if ready to strike.

"Wanna be like her, do ya?" The stick brushed beneath her knees.

Stunned, Martha felt something of his body beneath the cloth, something unfamiliar, and for a moment she was too surprised and frightened to move as his eyes narrowed and his mouth parted revealing stained bottom teeth. But then the bushes shook, parting, and Regina's dog reappeared, whimpering at first, then crouching and emitting a low, desolate growl. With that, Martha woke up. She pushed at Danny Qompt, trying to kick at him as he tightened his grip and raised his stick, but then he laughed and let her go. His laughter was a crooked, haughty sound.

She ran.

"Just like her," he called out. His voice stung with venal pleasure.

Running as fast as she could, Martha dared not look back. Only in the safety of her room did she stop, staring at her sisters folding laundry on their big double bed, such an ordinary, boring task. "Did you find it?" they asked, curious, patting smooth the sheets.

Martha didn't answer. She sat slumped on the other side of the bed, unable to speak. And yet, that night she pulled her hair back so tight, it made her eyes hurt.

"Old maid," Annie Laurie teased. She pressed her own eyes into slits so that her face looked blurred. The younger sister laughed.

Ignoring them, Martha knelt beside their bed. She had never tried to pray. She had never tried to sing hymns or to do anything religious other than to walk down the aisle to the altar. But tonight, she tried, she really needed to understand the slippery meanness beneath their lives. And yet the only words that came were "Help me."

Barely a week later, they heard the news. Regina had run away. She'd left at midnight, wearing her favorite lilac-colored shirt, the one she could no longer button and a grey wool skirt, the hem let down so that it covered her knees. She had no coat. No gloves. She wore work shoes, the same kind the men wore to the mines. That night, Martha lay awake in bed, unable to sleep, seeing Regina hurrying down the road, sneaking into the bushes when she saw someone, cramped and anxious and scared. There would be no notes in the bushes for her, no one around to worry about her loneliness. And then two days later, there was this: Regina had been found after midnight in the Birmingham bus station bathroom, her grey skirt soaked through with blood, her arms folded at her breast. She was dead.

Dead.

When the news spread through the classrooms at school, Martha couldn't move. She didn't cry or faint as some of the other girls did. She went still. Their hysterics, a chorus of wailing, came to her as if through a closed door. Though she felt stuck in time, her mind lurched, restlessly circling until it fixed on one horrible thought: Regina was alone when she died, alone and terrified. No one there. No one to call out her name.

Martha sank into shadow. She heard nothing, thought nothing as if she were no longer in the room, as if she were separate, invisible, as if she too could vanish.

She walked out into the cold.

When the new thought broke through, it was so unwieldy, she tried to push it away, but before she could censor it, it crystalized into a reckoning she felt too young to bear. *This was the hard path.* Not what had come before. That had been the short cut, the ordinary, vain choice of self-protection and delusion, the secret hope of avoiding tarnish, of being safe. Mrs. Qompt had never been her friend. Regina had needed her.

But what did this knowing matter if it came too late?

Everything too late. Martha opens her eyes, shifting her legs, easing the aching right one threaded with varicose veins, the blood pinched, the circulation cut off. At 94, she's sitting in her favorite white chair in her pretty kitchen. A rollator boxes her in and for a moment, she forgets why it's there. Then, she remembers: she has to use it to get up. To get out of her chair. She has to grip and *pull*. She'd meant to get up and make cheese straws for her great granddaughter to take to school tomorrow, but now the light is fading, and she's still boxed in, trapped in stillness, journeying down that dark road of memories.

She hasn't thought of Regina in years. And yet it was after Regina died that Martha lost her thirst for religion. She refused to go back to church where so much of that life had claimed her. She refused to go to Regina's grave. She refused, at first, to go to the funeral, but then at the last minute she crept into the very back pew so she could stare daggers at Mrs. Qompt—"Old Beady Eyes"—who sat in the front row decked out in righteousness. It was while Mrs. Curtis was playing the first rousing chords of "Amazing Grace" and the congregation standing to sing, that Ray Douglas slipped quietly into the back pew opposite Martha, a boy she hadn't seen in a long time. She sneaked glances at him. His face, still handsome and forlorn, looked thinner, shadowed after a year in the mines, the blue veins at his temples blurred by coal dust. He didn't seem to notice Martha. Tall and lanky, he still wore his stained work clothes as he sat hunched forward, his knees jutting out, his eyes closed. Only his hands moved, knotting and clenching as if he needed to smash something, but when he lifted his head, turning toward Martha, she was surprised to see that he was weeping. And then, all around her, the voices rose, deep-throated and tender, in a chorus of forgiveness, as old men and young lifted the casket and carried it carefully, humbly down the aisle and out the doors of the church.

Now Martha looks out her kitchen window. Darkness is near, the light fading. Yes, she needs to get up. She needs to straighten her legs, to walk, but she sinks deeper into stillness. "*I wander alone... I'm es drunk es the devil*," she whispers, the words oddly familiar, even comforting in her mouth as she stares at her bedroom slippers, a faded lilac bow perched on top. "Alone," she repeats and then she grips the walker with both hands and prepares to *pull*.

Jody Lisberger

HURRICANE BOB

An hour before the hurricane hits, Dad calls me on the phone. "Tape the windows," he says almost before he says hello. "Make a big X. With masking tape. Don't use duct tape. Whatever you do, don't use duct tape."

"Okay," I say, not letting on my surprise to hear his voice. I haven't spoken with him for two months. Not since he called me in June to say he was getting remarried.

I look over at the windows I've already taped. If my father were here, I'm sure he'd be showing me how to press every wrinkle and crease onto the glass. As if I don't know how to keep things from breaking.

"Be sure to fill everything with water," he booms in his get-out-there-and-play-like-you-mean-it voice. "Even the bathtub. Don't worry about the scum. Nobody needs to drink that water. Use it for flushing toilets." The last hurricane Dad was in, thirty-seven years ago, was Carol. It was 1954 and he was nine. He thought it was fun going with his father into the basement of their home. Seeing the water up to their shins, almost over their rubber boots. Throw rugs floating like Ali Baba's magic carpets.

"And whatever you do, Julien," he says, his voice suddenly dead serious, "don't touch the lights. I mean, if you're standing in water, don't *ever* touch the lights." I hear him pound his fist on the table like he's stamping something. Sealing it up.

I wonder if his new wife is sitting next to him.

"Okay, Dad," I say, knowing better than to remind him this isn't his summer house anymore.

"But if the water starts coming in—"

"I'm fine, Dad," I nearly shout into the receiver.

For a moment neither of us speaks. The birches on the far side of the lawn bend like women tossing hair over their heads. The sky turns a darker shade of solder gray. I picture him pinching his lips together, holding back what he really wants to ask. Not, *Is your Mother helping?*—though I'm sure he's tempted—but *When are you coming to visit me in Connecticut? Me and Nancy?*

It doesn't dawn on me yet that Mom might have called him to say she's stuck on the mainland. Worried about my being solo in the storm. Not used to the idea that I would be staying here without her. Not that I'm by myself. Though they don't know that.

In early July, Dad and Nancy were married in West Hartford by the Justice of the Peace. "The ceremony will be very quick and informal," Dad said when he called me mid-June in Honduras to share the big news. I was working with Habitat for Humanity between my junior and senior years of college. "No need to disrupt your commitment there," he said. "We'll celebrate when you get back." He didn't mention until the end of the conversation that Nancy was pregnant.

When I was three, I remember looking at the half moon, thinking my father could fix it. When I was ten, he was the one who picked me up from where I fell from a tree and rushed me to the hospital. He stayed up all night while we waited for the traction to lower my leg bones. At thirteen, he showed me how to uncurl a condom over a cucumber. No need to mention the word gay. Or AIDS. A few years earlier he'd brought them up, not that I was able then or for a long time to quiet my terror enough to do more than pretend he must have been talking about someone else. "Always use a condom," he warned this time. "And remember, whatever happens, I love you."

A week later I overheard him and my mother arguing. "He's too young to know for sure," she insisted.

"Just trying to be safe," he argued back. He made me promise to keep any talk of boyfriends out of the house until my mother "came round," he called it.

"So, what are your plans, now?" he asks, a waver in his voice.

I stare at the windows. I didn't realize they were so big until I started taping them. Like flags hoisted at the start of a sailing race. So big, boats from far away can see their warning. High winds. Proceed at your own risk.

"I'm going to fill the tub," I say, wondering if I'd ever ask him what happened to *his* condoms. Not very nice. I know. But I'm still dealing with the shock.

I wait to hear his usual response. Maybe the response I need to hear. *No need to be sarcastic, Julien. Nothing wrong with asking questions.*

In the silence, the line crackles, the ocean churns. Whitecaps rise as if to smash the fat silver X's on the windows. I should never have used duct tape. But it was all I could find.

Until I was fifteen, my mother, father, and I came to this Maine island off the coast of Portland every summer. Mom and I spent the whole season here, walking the paths through the woods and along the jagged rocks, loving the seclusion. No cars allowed on this summer-only island. She was an architect then, too. She would catch the island boat in and out of Portland to meet her clients. Off-season, she would sometimes drive to Portland, too. Dad, a public defender, came to the Island on weekends and for two weeks at the end of August, just when the light turned glossy and sharp. He and I loved to swim together in the freezing water. Loved how the numbness in our feet and legs made us feel like clunky old pilings, until we got out and the blood tingled back in. When I was little, I used to swim on his back, clinging to his neck as he dove under. He taught me early on never to violate the Eighth. Cruel and unusual punishment. Not that I understood amendments then.

Last March, when my parents told me they were getting divorced, we were sitting at our kitchen table in Connecticut after a late breakfast. It was the start of my college Spring Break. My mother had just arrived back from Portland. There was ice on the trees. I'd been out late the night before at a cast party for the Larry Kramer play I'd directed, *The Normal Heart*. Flowers from my friends stood in vases all around the house, the largest bouquets handed to me by my father, who'd come alone, not once but three times, to hear Ned Weeks plead with his lover, "Don't shut me out." Who'd hugged me after each show and whispered, "Great directing, Julien."

I'll never forget how nervous my mother looked as she sat down at the table.

"We have decided to get a divorce," she said.

My father stared at her as she spoke, his eyes fixed on her lips, as if they'd rehearsed beforehand. Him suggesting to her, "*Not "I have decided to get a divorce, but **We. We** have decided."*" In that moment, I wished our black lab was still alive. Thumping her tail against our legs. Asking to be loved.

Until my father's call in June, I thought I was the reason my mother wanted a divorce. They said "we," but I knew it was me. A gay son, unacceptable to her. *Irreconcilable differences.* Though I'd kept my promise to my father. Which made my life easier all those years. Or so

I thought.

Outside the rain begins to pelt the windows. Sideways slanting, swirling in squalls so thick for moments I can't see out. The wind howls, ripping off shingles from the old shed, clattering against the house. One of the birch trees snaps in half. An oak limb cracks and falls, snapping the power line, sparking as it crashes down. All hurricanes, three parts, I remind myself. The first part always the worst, the longest.

"You sure you'll be okay?" my father asks again, worry filling his voice.

"Dad, I'll be—"

"*Julio.*" Alex's whisper makes me turn my head, his Spanish "J," full of softness. He's standing in the master bedroom doorway holding a bucket. In Honduras we called him *Alejandro.* He's wearing his favorite T-shirt. A big red STOP sign on the front. "Tectonic plates" on the back. He lifts the bucket up and down. *Fill it?* I nod.

Three days ago, Alex and I ended up on the same flight from LaLima to LaGuardia. He was going to visit his family before heading out west to finish college. He said he'd never been to Maine. Could he come for a visit? Just a short visit? I thought he was joking. Until he showed up yesterday, despite the storm warnings.

"But if the rain starts coming in, who will help you?" Dad asks, the strain in his voice making clear to me where this is headed. *Where is your mother?* Not someone he's supposed to mention. And not someone he calls by name anymore. As if when you get divorced, the person you once loved loses their name forever.

"I'll be fine, Dad," I say again, deciding at the last second not to add "on my own." Why complicate things with a lie.

"But why isn't your Moth—?" He stops. "Sorry," he says. "*Sorry!*" He sounds almost angry at himself. "I just don't want you to be there all alone in the storm," he rushes on. "I want to be able to help—"

"But the boats aren't running," I add quickly, surprised at my panic. Imagine my father coming out here. Him and Nancy. In this house. With me and Alex and, for all I know, my mother if she were ever to arrive. "I have to go, Dad. Time to fill the—"

"Julien. Wait." His voice is deep and unwavering.

In that instant, I know what I should do. "Hang up," I tell myself. Two simple words. Two simple syllables. But I'm still listening as his chair scrapes on the floor and a door in his new house opens and closes.

"Julien," he says, his voice echoing as if he's in a garage now, or a pantry, cans of food lining the shelves. A white freezer hulking in the corner, waiting to be filled.

I look at the duct tape. It's going to be such a mess to pull off.

"What?" I speak softly. Out of courtesy and respect, I want to believe.

"Listen." His urgent quaver is back. "It's okay if you don't miss me right now. Or are angry at me. I understand that." He speaks quickly. "But I love you. I've always loved you. Even if things have changed and I—"

For a foolish second, I think he's going to apologize for getting remarried. For having a baby. For making me doubt everything I've believed about him. I hold my breath. Get ready to open my heart.

"I should never have let you miss the wedding. I should have insisted—"

"*Julio.*" Alex's voice is louder this time. He's pointing to the pots he's lined up on the counter in the wide opening between the kitchen and living room. All full of water. His eyes light up with the same glimmer he had when I told him last night the boats from Portland were cancelled.

"Dad, I have to—" I start to hang up.

"Don't you dare," he snaps. "If you do, I swear I'm coming out there this afternoon to get you myself. Hurricane and all. You hear me?"

Deep inside, the last thing I expect to feel is a burst of laughter welling up. The very idea of him driving three hours to come see me in a hurricane, too ridiculous for words. The highway, a skittery mess, the wind sideswiping the car. Nancy buckled in, the belt tight over her baby bump. And who the hell would bring them across the channel when my mother can't even find a prospect?

"Oh, Dad," I say, surprised to hear in my voice not laughter, or anger, but love. Can he hear that? Do I want him to hear that? Maybe he really is sorry. I look up to where Alex is standing beside the kitchen counter, as if listening to every word. He's holding a full bucket and grinning. He starts to rock playfully back and forth. To sing "Jack and Jill" just like we did to the little kids in the campo. "*Juan y Juanita . . .*"

I smile as I put my finger to my lips. "Shhhhhh."

On the phone there's a pause. "Jules?" Another pause. "You okay, kid?" But this time his voice has changed. Not stern and blunt, but low and raspy. The same way it used to be when I came up sputtering from those dives. When he would put on his goofy New Jersey trainer's voice, lift me on his shoulders, walk us through the water, and set me on the beach like I was a frozen toothpick. Toes first, skinny long legs, goose bumps all over my body. "You okay, kid?" he'd say, pretending to throw a few one-two punches before he wrapped me in a towel and wiped the sea water from my blinking eyes, his fingertips like cotton swabs, the salt water sharp on my sun-burned lips. Nothing like rainwater.

"You sure you're okay, Jules?" he asks again, his voice soft.

I take a deep breath. "Yeah, Dad," I say. For a moment, I almost believe I am.

And then it grows quiet. The rain stops. An eerie glimmer of light slivers along the distant horizon. Like the whole earth is taking a breath. *Don't be deceived by the eye of the storm*, I caution myself. I walk to the big windows. Touch the places where the old caulking has come loose. Water seeping through.

"Now what?" Alex calls from across the room.

"If we're lucky," I say, going to get some towels to put on the window sills, "the last part of the hurricane will be shorter and kinder. Will pummel the back of the house, not the front." Then I sit down at one end of the big sofa. In the corner, my father's boxes rise in a pile. Books and jars of sea glass. Lavender bottle stoppers, his greatest treasure. All of the boxes packed by my mother. Taped with duct tape.

Alex comes and sits on the other end of the sofa, as I know he will. In Honduras, he was the quiet and patient one, the kids always approaching him first. He smiles and nods, as if he understands those boxes, then pats the empty space between us. Gestures for me to move closer. "You look cold," he says. "Here." He takes the blanket looped over the back of the sofa and fluffs it out, as if I could hide behind it.

"No thanks, Alex," I say, surprised to find my words.

His brow wrinkles. "Why don't you call me *Alejandro*?" he asks quietly. "The way you said it down there. *Al-e-HAN-dro*."

Inwardly I sigh. I know what's coming next. Like one of the many scripts I've directed before. He reaches over. Puts his hand on my thigh. Not going anywhere. Just resting with his gentle touch. But just as gently, I lift his hand up and put it back on his leg, surprised at how easy this one gesture seems. Like passing a stack of poker chips from one person to another. Or closing a door quietly when someone is sleeping.

"This is different, Alex," I say, even though I love the sound of his name in Spanish, just as I love the sound of my name in Spanish. "We're *here* now." I pat the space between us like it's an ocean destined to keep islands apart.

"But I thought you liked me," he says quietly. He jiggles his legs the same way he did on the airplane.

"Of course, I like you," I could say, especially with his pensive eyes upon me. But I don't. Something about the banality of those words stops me. And something else, too. I can't get out of my mind the weird thought that my father might actually show up without Nancy. That he might come all this way to tell me I'm released from my promise. That if my parents have split, I no longer need to worry about my hurting my mother. He's already done that for me. Though I doubt he'd come right out and say so.

"I guess I'm just surprised you actually made it here," I say, biding my time as I try to untangle the feelings in my mind. *Why do I still feel I have to keep my promise to my father?*

"But you invited me," he says. He gets up and walks to the windows. Turns to face me. I wonder if he knows how the X's rise behind him like antlers.

"No I didn't," I say.

His face tightens. "Yes, you did. Why else do you think I came?" He gestures toward the white caps starting to rise again. "Because I *like* hurricanes?"

Inwardly, I have to smile. The truth is, I like the way his brow creases. The way all summer he's asked about my thoughts, my intentions, as if they matter. I like his dark curly hair, and the ease of his Spanish, even if he learned it, like me, in school. But for some reason, I need him to get his story straight.

"I didn't invite you," I say more sternly, thinking back to my words this past summer. *I'm not looking for a partner. Or a hook-up. My parents just divorced. I need time to clear my head.* Plus, in Honduras, what gay man would be crazy enough to hook up?

"You hear me?" I say, louder than I want or intend. "I didn't invite you. You decided to come on your—"

"Well, at least I decided," he says, his dark brown eyes boring into mine. Then without another word, he strides across the living room to the adjoining master bedroom where he slept last night. "I'm going to take a nap," he announces, not entirely nicely. "Wake me up when your goddamn hurricane is over."

For a long time, I sit on the sofa in the growing darkness. Of course, his words ring in my ears. *At least I decided.* For years, my indecision a way of protecting myself from letting the world—or is it myself—admit what I am. But this indecision is different, I want to say. Not about the desire to fuck or give an easy blow job—the first too fraught to imagine, the other too automatic to trust—but to tender my lips upon his lips, to explore the ins and outs around them, the intimacy of such closeness scarier than anything else. To be so deliberate and careful at once. Breath close. Warm. Why must this simple act seem so scary? As if my mother's house were holding me back? A tidy excuse.

Outside the wind starts to howl again. The rain batters the windows, not from the northeast, this time, but from the west. The birches behind the house crack and pop with each wailing gust. As the clouds thicken and swirl in looming columns, I imagine the roofs already peeled back in Portsmouth like the tops of tuna cans. The boats splintered on the rocks of Cape Anne. If I were the praying sort, I might pray my father would actually arrive. Tell me how glad he is to finally meet one of my friends. Encourage me to be who I am—as if letting go of my fears were as easy as diving into the coldest water and knowing, when you get out, you will soon warm up. I might also pray for a chance to redo that last scene. To tell Alex that of course I like him.

Last night, when I told him to sleep in the master bedroom, I said it was because I wanted him to have a view of the water when he woke up. Not like in my little bedroom on the lower level of this house. Only two small windows looking out at the birches, the sound of the waves always clear, but not in sight. He nodded as if he understood not only my desire to treat him well, but my need not to act too quickly. Maybe, too, he understands the odd prospect of being with a lover for the first time in your parents' house. Whether in their bed or yours. Whether kissing or fucking. Does that act destroy their power over you or reduce you to being just like them?

In the distance the whitecaps rise and smash against each other. The birch trees in the back scrape against the clapboards of the house. The kitchen screen door starts to bang. The wind too strong for the latch. I get up to pull the door tight. Grab some string from the kitchen drawer, thinking I'll rig up something to keep the door from ripping open and closed. As I get near, I don't expect to see a person hunched over on the back porch, their head bowed against the rain, the hood of their large yellow slicker concealing their face.

"Didn't you hear me knocking the first time?" my mother says in exasperation after I fling open the inside door. The brim of her hood sags down over her forehead. "And why was the door locked?" she asks as she reaches around the knob to undo the little inset. She glares at me. As if I knew the door was locked?

Too stunned to speak, I stand and stare at the rainwater running off her long slicker onto the kitchen tiles. One by one, she pulls apart the snaps, fans open the sides, then drops back the hood. If she wants me to comment on her haircut, or the two new gold studs in her right ear, she doesn't let on. Instead, she shakes her head, water pinwheeling everywhere (why is her hair wet?), then peels off the large slicker and holds it beside her like it might stand up on its own. Suddenly she laughs. "Can you believe this wind, this rain?" Her voice sounds giddy. Breathless. "I was so *lucky* to find David at DeMillo's." She pauses. "And so *lucky* he offered to bring me across the channel in his Whaler, so you wouldn't have to be here all alone!" She laughs again then pauses. Tilts her head as if waiting to see a light in my mind go on. "You remember my friend David, don't you?" She looks right at me, as if saying his name solves everything. "The guy whose house I designed six years ago? Who's come out to the island a few times to visit each summer?"

In that moment, indeed, a light bulb goes off. But not in the way I expect. I hear my mother lying, or at least stretching the truth. As if unlikely coincidences come out of nowhere. I *was* lucky *to find David at a floating restaurant in a hurricane?* Lucky *to find a ride across a roiling sea? Didn't have my own slicker, despite the forecast?* In that moment, I'm grateful she turns to hang her slicker on the hooks where we always hang our slickers. Glad she sees two slickers already there. Mine and Dad's, which I pulled out of a box for Alex to wear. Glad she can't see or feel the momentary joy of payback rising in me. *All this time, not my father but my mother has been the liar?*

"Honey?" she says, pausing mid-reach. There's a tremble in her voice. "Is—" she points to Dad's slicker. "Is your Fa—?" But here she stops, as if to check herself. My father—would he break the rules? Or maybe because she hears the master bedroom door crack open and, just as quickly, though far more quietly, close, sparing me from having to explain why Alex is not only here, but naked, or wearing only boxers, or wrapped in Dad's bathrobe, which we found in the back of the closet. (And what will I say when he *does* walk out? *Remember my friend Alex, who happened to come to the island yesterday?*)

"Oh, Jules," my mother groans as she turns toward the living room. I brace myself for the obvious question. *Who's in the master bedroom?* But without another word she marches to the big windows and, with her nails, picks at one of the silver X's. Peels it back a little. Gunk stuck to the glass. "How could you?" she groans again.

So many things I could say. *Dad told me to use duct tape. Dad knew you'd hate it. Dad knew it would be impossible to get off.* Or maybe just, *Where are your flowers for me?* But instead, I take a deep breath, walk over to the sofa, sit down, and pat the empty cushion beside me. I wait for my mother to join me. So much for distant oceans.

I start slowly. "You mean you're glad I taped the windows with whatever I could find?" I pause. *No need to be sarcastic, Julien.* "Glad I had the smarts to gather water?" *Nothing wrong with asking questions.* I gesture toward the kitchen counter as if I filled those pots myself. "You mean, *thank you for all your efforts?*" I turn and look right at her, bracing myself for the hard crease down the middle of her brow when she gets angry if I talk about the choices in my life she doesn't want to hear.

She lowers her head, pinches her lips together. "Sorry, Jules," she says quietly. "I didn't mean to criticize. And I didn't mean—"

"—to keep your secret about David forever?" I say in a whisper, not because I want to whisper, but because my heart is racing so fast that's all that comes out. That, and a most unexpected wish that Alex would walk out right now, with all his clothes on, extend his gentle hand, and greet my mother with the simplest of all greetings. *Buenos tardes, Senora. Me llamo Alejandro. ¿Como esta?*

But the banging of the screen door makes both of us whip our heads around. My mother gets up quickly. I know who will be there. Enough time for David to have tied up his boat on the cove side of the island. To have walked over in the pelting rain. Without his slicker. I confess my wish in that moment is not nice. For her to find not David at the door, but Dad. Dad by himself. No Nancy, or baby, or flowers.

No one is there.

"It must have been the last of the wind talking," my mother says, coming back to sit beside me. She pulls the fuzzy blanket onto her lap. Points to the X's on the clearing windows. "I was only meaning to show concern for the work it will take us to clean the glass," she says. She pauses. "Why, when your father and I were little and unknown to each other, I remember how hurricanes came sweeping through. How your father loved to tell the story of carpets floating. How your father—"

"His name is Nathan," I say very quietly, surprised at how much I need to say his name and have her say it, too.

"You don't need to tell me Nathan's name, Jules." Her voice is barely audible, maybe even a little sad. "I was married to him for twenty three years. I loved him for much of that time, and he loved me back. In case you needed to know." She pauses to wipe a drop of rainwater running down her neck. "Dad knew about David all along, Jules." She pauses. "He also wanted us to stay together until you were ready to go your separate way, too." She gazes at the X's, then back at me, tilting her head as if her ears, like my ears, are perked to hear a door opening. "Now, Jules, is there anything else you want to tell me?"

Mrinal Rajaram

In Second Person

You pull out the diary from underneath a large pile of books and write these words:

November 1

We build walls. Walls that encircle us. High walls. Walls that we delude ourselves into believing cannot be scaled. Walls to protect us from attack, vulnerability, pain. Little do we know that all it takes is a single, seemingly inconsequential moment, for that fortress to be breached. When those walls come crumbling down, you understand that you are a long way away from being all right. Far from the reassuring comfort of false contentment, false happiness. To experience vulnerability is to experience an indescribable incompleteness. A feeling of nakedness on display.

Your defences wane. It is almost better to feel nothing as opposed to its opposite. Something possesses the capacity to cause you harm. Nothing does not. Love. Unrequited. One-sided. Call it what you may. An emotion that can be likened to having your insides wrenched out, and being made to witness them being stomped on with the full weight of heavy feet. When it surrounds you with its pervasive presence, you might not have the ability to protect yourself from being affected by it. Where are those walls now?

Four days pass. Another entry:

November 5

When you haven't as much as held a person's hand for many years, you begin to comprehend the value of human contact. The need for bonding. The need for having someone to listen, without the fear of being judged. To share the things that cannot be shared. You think you had it once, long ago. You can't be sure. Some people find intimacy easily. Why is it so hard for you, then?

You observe many of the people you grew up with. Their keenness for life is more apparent than yours. You see enough satisfaction in their manner to believe that it is, perhaps, worth it. Some of them are beginning to settle down, others in relationships that are leading to some place of stability. You wish them well. But when you witness them from close quarters, you bring into question the choices that have brought you to this point. It is not envy. Longing is probably what it is. Hard to tell. Getting married is not all it is cracked up to be—hasn't he received a valuable lesson in that regard from his parents? What is key, is forging a connection with someone who is willing to understand and accept the complicated brokenness that resides within. And for you to reciprocate the same. But who, in reality, would wish to take on that pile of burden and trauma that is you? Is it just to put another human being in that position?

You are jaded, having unconsciously lost the power or ability to feel anything of consequence over the last few years. Filling voids with all the things you do possess to compensate for all the things you don't, doesn't seem to be working out for you as well as it used to.

Confronting the deepest, darkest part of the self scares you out of your wits. You do this sitting in a corner, all by yourself, sometimes. Waiting. Reflecting. Friends and family not having the slightest inkling of what is raging inside. Too afraid to tell them, as usual. All the things that make you get up in the morning—your writing, your exercise, your books, your music—seem to matter less when you have dug yourself into a hole. Could that be the real definition of giving in?

You force yourself to venture beyond the four walls. Moping will get you nowhere. You tap into that streak of black humour. You laugh. You laugh at yourself. You make others laugh. Laughter is good. Funny boy! Going out and pretending that all is well is not nearly as easy as it seems. It is not a conscious effort to pretend. It is something that happens without you realising.

You attempt to come to terms with these traits in the confines of your solitude. You have had an inkling of their existence for some time now. But their real meaning has somehow escaped scrutiny.

The lines border on the sentimental, you are aware. But there is a certain truth even to sentimentality.

You go into work one day. You have not been in, in a while. Your assignments get filed from home, as they have always been. You notice a new face as you enter but pay no heed to it. The ensuing half hour is spent in catching up with colleagues, discussing the latest features and developments, office goings-on, a quick hello to the editor. The usual.

You are introduced to *her* by a short-haired colleague, a friend. Fresh out of university with a degree in journalism and politics, she is visiting from halfway across the world. Interning in the land of her birth. She tells you that this is her last week in the city. She leaves for another place, and then another, before she ultimately heads back home. You remember the minute details well, as if it were yesterday. The scarf, the dark jeans, the distinct nose, the long tapering fingers, the ponytail, a favourite book, her fondness for narrative nonfiction and longform journalism. The fawn sandals with thin soles, their delicate straps separating each foot's larger toe from the other smaller ones, convince you of her simple, yet elegant sense of style. You gauge enough from the chat to detect interest. You may have been wrong about such instances in the past. But instinct tells you otherwise. For a handful of solitary seconds, you wish that you had dressed a little better that day.

Once the small talk is over, the conversation switches seamlessly to the art of writing, and creativity. This carries on for the next half hour. Your short-haired-colleague-friend is also an integral part of the exchange. You express an opinion that creativity is something that cannot be taught. Even a spark of it can be harnessed, but not taught from scratch. She mulls it over, choosing to listen instead. You go on to speak of the subjectivity of the form. She responds by saying that "there is good and bad writing, though." You agree with that statement, in essence, but believe that even good and bad, in case of the written word, are subjective entities—open to interpretation. An additional discussion is had on reading as the primary source of inspiration for the writer. There is no clear sign of telling whether the two of you are in agreement. Before you depart, she tears a neat piece of paper from a notebook, writes down the address of her email and blog, and hands it over. She would be pleased to read your work, she says. You never usually share your fiction with people you are unfamiliar with. But you wish to make an exception this time.

Hours after you have left the office, for some inexplicable reason, the vision of her scarf keeps playing over and over in your mind. The garment's dizzyingly intricate pattern comes to memory without difficulty, but it is the juxtaposition of colours that evades you.

Late at night, back home, in the familiarity of your bare room, you visit the WordPress site. You read two or three of the most recent entries. For someone just out of college, she sure has a great deal of perspective. The intelligence is quite clearly discernible. Not only are you taken in by the pristine style, but it is the social commentary, the profound observations, the painstaking detail, of certain aspects of a country that must be so alien, so complex, so contradictory to her, that keep you riveted. There is a kind of power, a force, that resonates from the words, the syntaxes, the sentences. You are unable to express your thoughts about it with ease. From what little you have read; you feel a strong sense of wanting to belong. The command over language is one of her many fortes.

You go over more posts as the days trudge along. The writing cuts your heart with the exacting precision of a sharpened blade. It strikes your conscience with an honest sensitivity that you have rarely encountered before from such a young writer. You wish you could articulate your thoughts as lucidly. There are undertones of melancholy that flow through the narrative. You fail to place a finger on it, but it is embedded there somewhere, subtly.

There are those writers, by a close examination of their work, you know, have the potential to make it very far in life.

In the process of reading and rereading you get an insight into what she might be like as a person, the voice behind the words. Strong, decisive, and self-assured, yet receptive to the larger world that she is indeed a part of. *An admirer of beauty. An idealist. An aesthete.* Aren't we all, in some small way, a product of our words?

You share with her your opinions in a series of emails—the first of which gets sent a day after you have met her. The messages are detailed, full of true admiration. She replies, thanking you, and asks about the stories you had promised. You write back, assuring her that the work will be sent. You have been busy tying up loose ends ahead of your friend's wedding that takes place in a city by the seaside in under a week's time. You venture to ask if she would like to meet. You are being more forward than usual. She declines politely, stating that she will be travelling very soon. She uses the word *unfortunately* in her response. The next time, perhaps, is all you can say in return.

You send her five of your stories in the days that follow. In the weeks that have passed since you first walked into office, you have emailed her many links and web pages relating to literary magazines and their submission guidelines, articles on creative writing, and the like. *Months of research.* She reciprocates by mailing three of her poems, apart from a link that discusses the cult of authenticity in Indian fiction writing by Vikram Chandra. The piece in the *Boston Review* dates as far back as early 2000. It is a long, analytical essay that begins with three Indian writers, including Chandra, onstage, for a book reading at the British Council in

Delhi. One of the writers receives a question from the audience about a passage in his book, that describes in great detail, the process of preparing bhelpuri on a busy Bombay by lane, as his young protagonist looks on, amazed. Chandra feels impelled to add his two cents. He waits for his counterpart to respond, and then, in his crisply fluent style, says to the gathering, "To delight in the mundane is what an artist does." The line makes a searing impression on you.

She will share specific feedback on the work with you. It will take some days. *That's no matter.* She is still in the country, but no longer in town. You tell her that you are no connoisseur of poetry, but will read hers, regardless, and get back with your thoughts.

The third entry:

December 9
You ask yourself why the powers that be end up being cruel. Why did you have to meet her at a time when she was all set to leave? Why did you have to meet her at all, for that matter? Is there any proper way of telling someone who lives at the other end of the world that you are drawn towards their art ... drawn towards them? There isn't. Besides, you could not possibly know how they perceive you. There is a strong part of you that wishes, by some stroke of providence, she does not leave the country soon. What that will achieve, exactly, there is no way of telling.

Her thoughts on your fiction arrive gradually, as promised. She compliments you on the imagination, the intimate knowledge of your characters and their circumstances, and the embedding of small details in the narrative structure. There are two critical points she wishes to discuss. The first, being the application of too much *tell* in the work. *Show me more, tell me less,* is about the gist of it. This analysis is undertaken by highlighting the contrast between two distinct paragraphs from your longest story. She would prefer that the social construct of the pieces unfold through its characters' lives and influences around them instead of being stated directly to the reader. The second, is what she perceives to be a dearth of conflict in the stories. There is perhaps one story that may have some conflict within it, nevertheless. Hence, she considers the work more vignette than short story, for the most part. You are appreciative of the candid observations. However, you do not concur with the entire feature of the critique. You have your own views about the notion of conflict in your work. You express these very thoughts in the extended reply. In it, you reference the typical Chekovian story structure that lacks a moral finality, while blurring the traditional lines of a clearly mapped out beginning, middle, and end. You also convey the opinion that, conflict, in your fiction, is primarily internal—in the minds of your characters. *An aspect which she alludes to, no doubt.*

You detect a hint of disappointment from her analysis. *A feeling that she was expecting more, somehow.* That makes two disappointed people, then. You cannot help but admit that you were looking forward to a more enthusiastic response. Not to be. But you do commend the honesty.

The length of your reply is twice as large as her feedback email. You did not originally intend to write this much but are too invested in it to back away now. There is a passing mention of the short fiction works of Tolstoy, Tagore, Wilde, Maupassant, and O Henry. *How Much Land Does a Man Need? The Kabuliwala, The Model Millionaire, The Diamond Necklace, The Last Leaf.* How Chekov inspired generations of writers after him—from Hemingway to Munro to Lahiri. No matter how it appears, you aren't trying to come across as *a know-it-all, an armchair intellectual, a fake.* You have much to learn, yet. It is only your passion for literature that has set you off thus. In hindsight, you may well have checked yourself. But once the send button gets pressed, there is no turning back.

The correspondence on her part, in particular, is of a semi-formal nature. What one would employ with a mere acquaintance. Nothing in it that can be construed as interest. Your initial instinct seems to have been false, after all. The insight gives you a sharp twinge.

You hold on to that thin, fragile strip of handwritten paper. It buries itself deep within the recesses of your consciousness. It may sound absurd, but it is almost the same as hanging on to a part of someone you do not wish to let go. *Someone you hardly know.*

You fret over something untoward that might have slipped out in the messages. Thoughts that have succeeded in putting her off. *Appeared too eager, perhaps.* These are only hunches, of course. The emails start dwindling till she ceases to reply altogether. In the meantime, you have sent her an additional two stories that have been edited recently.

As expected, they go unanswered. Perhaps an eventual answer is in the offing, but how long must you wait until you are absolutely certain that there is none forthcoming?

Another mail finds its way into your inbox. From a literary journal that you submitted three fiction pieces to, more than a year ago. It has almost faded from memory. The short note reads:

Dear submitter,
We appreciate your patience in hearing back from us. Your work has received careful consideration, but we regret to inform you that it is not a right fit for the magazine at this time. We wish you all the best in placing it elsewhere.
Regards,
The Editors
* Note—please do not reply to this email

In order to make it as a writer, it is imperative for you not to take literary rejection personally.

The diary makes its appearance for one final time:

February 21
Days pass you by. Unmotivated days. You fail to distinguish one from the other. The sameness of the everyday. You remain rooted to the apartment. Rejecting all external influence. A cloistered existence. Getting out of bed, following any kind of regular routine, become heavy chores. There is a drastic drop in appetite. When you do manage to eat, it is mostly junk. You let the facial hair grow out beyond the usual length. You brush your teeth only late into each day if you brush at all. You bathe infrequently. You ignore calls. All you feel is this intense loss of energy that prevents you from being productive. The classic signs of depression.

You return to that familiar place of emptiness. Odd, how a stray moment or two has the power to take you back to square one. It stares you in the face, as clear as day.

If this keeps up any more than usual, it won't be long before you find yourself in the not-so-reassuring confines of a therapist's office. Right on.

You opt for an indefinite leave of absence from work, citing concerns of ill health. Fortunately for you, your boss is a considerate lady. You pour through the channels on TV in the hope of some divine intervention in the form of entertainment. You are not a regular watcher unless it entails sport. At every flick of the remote, the crassness of reality television invades your senses. An infamous windbag who identifies himself as the voice of the people (and perhaps the voice of reason too), berates a volatile guest on a nightly talk show. This sensationalistic claptrap being projected is ostensibly the news. *Objective journalism be damned! Even if that concept is said to exist only in theory.* You cringe with disgust until an advertisement for a Guru Dutt film feature on *Zee Cinema* catches your fancy. *Evenings With Dutt Sahib* will present one film of the auteur every night for the next seven nights. You have always wished to see the man's cinematic creations. Ray, Sen, Ratnam, Nair, Mehta, Kashyap, Bhardwaj. You have borne witness to all these parallel cinema greats of the ages. But somehow, Dutt has remained in the shadows. Ghatak, Gopalakrishnan, and Balachander are yet to be explored, and possibly even marvelled at. You stash a mental note away for safekeeping.

Pyaasa and *Kaagaz Ke Phool* come highly recommended. By virtue of their critical standing, they feature as one and two on the list. You watch them on successive nights. You are almost moved to tears by their sheer genius. *The soulful melody of Burman, the inimitable Waheeda Rehman, myriad emotions flowing from Dutt's troubled face, deft subtleties in cinematic technique, the unmistakable sensitivity in every frame.* You soak them all in, as one would do in a trance. You do not recollect seeing a woman appear this exquisite when she breaks into a frown, as Rehman often does in each of the films. *The iconic Waheeda frown! Pyaasa* clutches to the strings of your heart refusing to let go, but it is *Kaagaz Ke Phool* that succeeds in breaking it. You hold them both in high regard, but it is the latter that makes a more lasting impression. The crushing impact of the finale has something to do with it, perhaps. *Sahib Bibi Aur Ghulam* and *Chaudhvin Ka Chand* are also part of the retrospective. Though these two films feature Dutt as actor and producer, it is understood that he contributed heavily to the creative process. Abrar Alvi, his trusted screenwriter and confidante, would later find himself embroiled in a controversy that alleged it was Dutt who had, in reality, directed *Sahib Bibi Aur Ghulam.* These claims have never been substantiated, and are, in all probability, false.

Guru Dutt was a man who made commercial films in his early days so as to enable him to remain true to his art when the time and circumstance were right. That initial phase of toeing the line would lead up to his first real masterpiece, *Pyaasa*, in 1957. It is a wonder that *Kaagaz Ke Phool* fared miserably at the box office when it was released to audiences for the first time, two years later, thanks in part to the film's depressive elements and unhappy conclusion. After the critical and commercial achievements of *Pyaasa, Kaagaz Ke Phool* (that shared many similarities with its more illustrious predecessor) was expected to do well. But that was not to be the case. The film would rise from the depths of neglect and ruin to become a cinematic classic the world over decades after Dutt's unfortunate passing. *Ironic.* Artists often speak to you about their life through the medium of their work. The end to the man's short existence should have come as less of a shock to the people of this country. The signs were there for all to see.

Much to your annoyance, you are unable to watch the other films in the feature for some reason or other.

Your habitual reading rituals have stalled for a time. You are forced to revisit them to keep your mind from the largely unhealthy practice of over-thinking. The over-thinking must be reserved for the days of putting pen to paper. *Not today.* After much deliberation, you pick up *The Wind-Up Bird Chronicle.* It has been lying on the bookshelf, unread, for months. This is your sixth Murakami novel in less than two years. You are what can be termed an ardent admirer. *What is it that attracts you so much to his work?* His withdrawn, disengaged, alienated characters, you believe, are perhaps shades of the enigmatic writer himself. *Conjecture.* But one can always make a calculated guess.

Book One: "The Thieving Magpie," June and July 1984
Chapter One: Tuesday's Wind-Up Bird, "Six Fingers and Four Breasts"
You commence reading. The narrative pulls you magnetically in to its surrealist fold as much of his work has succeeded in doing up until this point.

Your two musical companions on this lonesome journey of the mind are "Jhoom Barabar Jhoom Sharabi" (Janab Aziz Nazan's famed 1970s

qawwali from *Five Rifles*) and "I Wanna Be Yours" from Arctic Monkeys'
most recent album, *AM*. A stark contrast in melodic styles, if any. The
lyrics of each song resonate with a poignant truth you are bound to
connect with. That is all they will ever have in common. *"Secrets I have
held in my heart, are harder to hide than I thought,"* sings Alex Turner.
The track sets to music John Cooper Clarke's poem of the same name.
Its animated video matches the song's vision near perfectly. You have
recommended this number to her a few days prior. *The last straw. The
straw that broke the camel's back. Poor camel!* You are left to only wonder.

You stand on your small balcony, overlooking the road below. Bare-
chested, in shorts, you observe with curiosity, the world goes by.
Observation, you understand, is an essential characteristic of the creative
process. This activity is carried out for days, with little respite. There are
mental images of future stories forming in your brain, of people passing
by—some, if not all of them. The same darkness that will someday
destroy you is the same darkness that makes you acknowledge the light.
Your unwavering faith in the power of the written word. Slowly but surely,
you are regaining the need to attempt fiction again. You are too dreary
to begin just yet. And it may not sound like much. But the need for it is
always a good start.

Lynn Gordon

THE ONYX BRIDGE

On their thirty-third anniversary they went for a hike in the Painted Desert, which lay some distance from their hotel in Winslow. Clare knew herself to be the athletic one—strong and lean from jogging and exercise classes—and it seemed a great concession that, after two hours of driving through the national park and pulling over at each point of interest, Howard was willing to walk cross-country into the desert with her.

Really, Howard had insisted on every little stop. First the visitor center at the south end, where he lingered over the fossil of a phytosaur, then the Long Logs trail, where he gazed upward from the trailhead and announced that he could make out a few of the petrified logs. "I don't need to get closer," he'd said. "It's kind of chilly to go wandering off."

But now, apparently through a sales job by a ranger, they were scrambling down a path into the heart of things. Below them, and far into the distance, were hills of sand in red and yellow layers. Trackless land, seemingly plantless, under a sapphire sky. After the downhill stretch, they followed a worn path that quickly faded.

Two weeks earlier, when Clare had told her sister about the impending trip to Arizona, Jackie had quirked her mouth. "Hope springs eternal?"

"Well, maybe. You don't have to tell me. But I'd like to see the place."

Jackie laced her fingers in her lap, stuck out her elbows. "I was thinking of your last trip."

"Believe me, that crossed my mind, enough to wear a rut through it. Here's my logic: We're not exactly compatible at home; this won't be worse. And, as I said, I've never been. I want to go."

Jackie's eyebrows pushed upward and held.

Clare shrugged. "What if the trip is lousy? Then I might finally be ready."

"You mean... ?"

"I mean."

Treading the vast sands, Clare at last felt inklings of freedom and celebration. She touched Howard's arm briefly. "Tell me again what the ranger said."

"There's a place called Onyx Bridge. He says it's fantastic. Lots of petrified wood out there."

He withdrew a folded paper from his hip pocket and opened it to show Clare a map of sorts, squiggled with topo lines, and a "suggested route." "Should be a piece of cake to find it. We start by going north." From his breast pocket he took a compass.

Whatever anyone might say about Howard, he was a whiz with topo maps. Early in their marriage, when they lived in San Jose, he would lead them cross-country through the Sierra's forests and granite slopes.

Referring now and then to the slip of paper, Howard pounced his way through the sands. Clare followed, immersed in the pinks and reds anchored by lead-blue. She let herself think, as she had more and more lately, about life on her own—at large in a new world like this one. That brought her back to the moment, and she tried to let go her exasperation of the past few hours. This, after all, was the cream of the day.

The wind blew and the air glittered. Howard muttered something about Lithodendron Wash, a name that Clare had noticed on the map. This was like the old Howard. The current, fifty-eight-year-old Howard was borderline diabetic, with a mound of belly pushing out his shirt. At home he liked to lounge around with one of his heavy volumes, tossing out unasked-for facts and—sometimes—peevishly correcting her grammar.

They walked further; the day lost its morning chill. Howard turned and pulled Clare by the elbow. He pointed to a dot in the sky. "A redtail." Clare reflected on this skill he had always had, of spotting distant creatures and knowing what they were.

Howard rubbed a hand over his forehead and balding scalp. "You didn't bring a hat," Clare said. She was never without her own, which crushed down to fit into a pocket.

They came to a small declivity and stumbled downward. "Lithodendron Wash, I presume." Howard pointed ahead. "Look out there. A couple of vultures."

Clare glanced and murmured, but vultures were not a rare sight. She turned to see behind her, to search out the way they had come. She fixed on a high point on the rim; that would guide them back when the time came. At the same time, she noticed that she and Howard were alone, except for one faraway figure just starting down the path they had taken.

Howard looked back, too. "We're a ways out already. Let's follow the wash, along to the right."

"It's not the wrong direction? Longer, I mean."

"Longer but easier."

On they went, Clare pausing now and then to close her eyes and sniff the air, feel the sun. Out here, in the full-but-empty heart of the desert, energy coursed through her body. The horizons urged her forward, asked her to go infinitely far.

But Howard—he seemed to slow with every step. She had to hold herself in check to keep from outpacing him.

She looked back toward the rim again and was surprised to see a man quite close behind her, probably the same person she had spotted before, who had been so far away.

Seeing her turn, the man waved sheepishly. He was really a boy, Clare could see now, a boyish-aged man. "You going to Onyx Bridge? Is this the way?" He held a small electronic gadget, at which he shook his head. "Can't quite figure this out."

By this time Howard had also turned to look at the boy. For the merest moment, Clare allowed herself to compare the two of them. The boy: rangy and white-toothed, a bit like the old Howard. Her eyes lingered on his free hand—the one not holding the GPS—on its long fingers and deftly grooved knuckles. And then Howard, as he was now.

Howard gestured toward a series of dunes to the left. "It's that way. We're taking the scenic route."

The boy came closer. "I'll just follow you, then." Not really a question.

Clare and Howard exchanged a glance. "All right," said Clare. She and Howard continued along the wash, where water sometimes had run, sometimes in a torrent. She had to imagine it as she walked over what seemed absolute dryness. Streaks and riffle marks everywhere, but they were fossils to Clare. The water might have come through decades or centuries before.

Turning her head, she saw the boy from the corner of her eye. He had dropped back a hundred feet but still followed her. Her and Howard, of course.

Howard came to a stop, there in the sand. He wiped his forehead with the back of his wrist.

"Drink some water," said Clare. She knew she must be perspiring, too, but the desert air sucked it away before she could feel it. "It's beautiful, right?"

He stared at the dunes off to their left and squeezed his lips. A tinge of smile. "More your kind of beauty than mine. I was never a desert rat." He took out his water bottle and drank, handed it to Clare. "Still," he conceded.

For Howard, this was generous behavior. As they went on, Clare thought of their last trip. Howard had bought tickets to B.C. without consulting her. They arrived in Victoria in early December, where Howard indulged his gusto for museums, leaving Clare to purchase an umbrella and patrol the rainy streets. Darkness came early. On the third day he convinced her to join him for Butchart Gardens. She remembered endless paths through the many unblooming gardens, sleet cutting her cheeks, while Howard loitered in the cold and examined bare branches with a botanist's eye.

Howard's slowness was prolonging their walk, for which she was happy. The sun beat deliciously through her shirt. A womb warmth, she thought; this must be what it is like.

She looked to see if the boy was gaining on them; he had closed the gap only a little. He was really very young. For a ridiculous instant, she felt gladness that a young, handsome man was following them.

The wash curved to the left and to the left again. The afternoon heat enfolded Clare's shoulders and arms, puffed around her legs in the breeze. A striped lizard scuttled across the sand. Howard kept on.

She had come down with fever after Butchart Gardens. Howard had left her to twist within the damp sheets of their hotel bed while he immersed himself in . . . was it the Maritime Museum? He set her up with a cup of tea before he left, and an extra blanket from a drawer. Hours later he returned, raving about dugouts or some frigging thing.

"I need aspirin. I'm at a boil."

"You should have seen their collection." Howard had stood beside the bed, his face hanging over hers. "I wish you'd take an interest."

"Can you go buy some aspirin?"

"Right now? It's raining." But he went.

When he came back, dripping bogs onto the figured carpet, he tossed the aspirin bottle so that it landed next to her ankle. "Do you know what kind of a storm is out there? The place was, like, ten blocks away."

The sun, brighter than before, only made the colors more engulfing. The desert became a colossal blanket, with lumps and bumps and stripes rippling everywhere, upon which three small creatures made their way.

The wash bent to the right now, and Howard led the way up the bank. He and Clare stopped to inspect the map on the ranger's leaflet. The boy came up behind them and stood surprisingly close; Clare could see the slight crookedness of his white teeth. A birth mark blotched the skin in front of his ear.

"Hi," he said. Clare gave him a careful smile.

Howard held the leaflet in front of Clare and gestured toward a flock of dunes. "It's in there, up one of these winding little passages. We'll find it."

The boy said, "I'll stick close. If that's okay."

"Well, actually," said Howard, addressing the boy for the first time, "it's our anniversary. We might like a little privacy. If that's okay."

The boy seemed unfazed. He dropped back a few yards and continued to follow them.

When Clare had talked to her sister two weeks earlier, Jackie said, "It's not all bad, is it? Don't be . . . you know, don't be hasty."

"Thirty-three years isn't hasty." As she spoke, Clare knew the unfairness of the comment. She had said it to be witty, a reflex.

"Exactly. You guys are two of a kind, aren't you? You wouldn't have stuck around for so long without any reason."

Clare had felt herself prickling, all over her shoulders and cheeks and neck. "You're my sister, not God."

Regrettably, that had ended the visit.

They headed into a gully between two dunes and soon reached a dead end—a jumble of rocks and sand. "But look at all the logs," said Howard. "They look just like wood, only ..." He clambered a short way upslope to rap his knuckles on one. "Solid! They're stone."

Clare came up next to him and bent to stroke the log. "Something that looks like what it was but isn't anymore." The words amused her. "Or did I say that wrong?"

"It was a jungle here," said Howard. "Only a few hundred million years ago."

They walked back through the gully, passing the boy, who waved his hand as they went by. Howard ignored him and forged across the sands to another opening between dunes. Here the petrified wood lay thick around them, long, heavy logs and shattered bits. Clare marveled to herself as she stepped around rocks and felt her shoes dig into the sand.

"Really lush back then." Howard seemed to have read her mind. "And now . . ."

"Grasses."

Their passageway forked, and Howard hesitated before choosing a branch.

The Onyx Bridge lay off to one side, eight or ten feet below them. Despite its myth-evoking name, the Bridge consisted of a plain brown petrified log, part of which spanned a narrow wash. Howard had had to point it out, or Clare wouldn't have noticed.

She didn't mind; it was the walk that mattered, the wild sky and the desert. Howard moved a little way off and began trudging up a purple and white hillock. Clare hung back, assessing the great prize, the Onyx Bridge. It had once been a mighty tree.

The boy, never far behind, had scrambled down to the Bridge and begun a photography session. Holding out his telephone camera, he snapped the log from every angle. At last, he stood on it to take a few shots of himself as conqueror.

Clare untied the bandana from around her neck, wiped her sunglasses, and reknotted the bandana. She moved quickly to catch up with Howard, and the two of them sat down just over a rise, where they could gaze at the landscape, their backs to the Onyx Bridge.

They shed their day packs and took out the lunch: apples, tomato-provolone sandwiches, and jerky from a roadside stand. "Look at this view," Clare said. Then she peeked back over her shoulder. The boy was still there, mucking around the Onyx Bridge. Probably waiting for her and Howard to guide him back.

Howard bit hard on a strip of jerky and then chewed. He ate with zest. When he spoke, it was to continue their earlier conversation, from before they had found the Bridge. "It seems like only grasses, but lots of plants grow here. They've adapted to the desert."

She mulled that.

"See this thing?" Howard put out one finger and hovered it over a tiny, branching plant. "See the bud? The other stalks are going to bud, too."

She set down her sandwich and bent far to the side to examine

Howard's plant: thin, grayish leaves and one undeniable budlike growth. Trust Howard to appreciate the minutiae.

It had been so different in the past, before the trees fell over and petrified. Yet life—a sort of microlife—was going on even now. As she sat back up, he brushed his hand down her arm.

After the sandwiches, Howard reached into his pack and took out something in gold foil.

"What's that?" Clare leaned over to peer at it. "You brought chocolate? In the desert?"

"Hell, it's our anniversary." Howard tore the edge of the package, which buckled at his touch. He showed Clare the contents—a brown muck that adhered to the foil.

Clare burst out laughing, and eventually Howard, who could be slow to see humor, brayed out loud. As he stowed the mess in his pack, he looked back toward the Bridge. "Damn kid's still around. Let's go off into that gully over there, get away from him."

It felt deliciously childish, waiting until the boy was looking elsewhere, then sneaking off into a hidden fold of the land. They flopped down and Clare leaned back against the slope.

"Waiting like some kind of buzzard," declared Howard. "A bloodsucking freeloader."

She giggled. "Buzzards don't suck blood."

"Whole new kind."

She closed her eyes and then opened them. "But really, how were there trees . . . and everything else?"

"Here? This was the tropics back then. It's all shifted."

Shifted—a mind-bending feat of geologic time. Hundreds of millions of years ago, a jungle populated by enormous phytosaurs. Today they had seen only one small lizard. She drowsed for a while in the sand.

When she woke, she found Howard staring into the narrow stretch of sky above them.

"You missed a golden eagle. Huge wings. I noticed by the shadow passing over."

Clare sat upright. "You should have waked me up."

He shrugged. "You were snoozing. Come on, let's go back."

As they came to the Onyx Bridge, Clare looked for the boy and felt a strange relief at not finding him. He must have headed back on his own.

Howard broke into her thoughts: "Do him good to work it out by himself, to the extent he can with that gizmo calling the shots."

She found herself suddenly irritated. "It should be dead easy for *anyone* to aim back toward the rim and find the path up."

"Ha. You're assuming initiative that may not be there."

When they emerged from the gully, she scanned the desert, the grasses and sand and the wash. The sun had grown hotter; the land pulsed under its brightness. No human silhouette broke the rich continuum before her.

Howard turned, and she saw that his scalp and cheeks had grown red. "We'll take our time," he said. Another statement that was—or was not?—like him.

Clare untied her neckerchief and held it out. "Take it," she said, when he did nothing. Finally, he folded the kerchief over his scalp and knotted it at the back.

She wondered again that Howard had come without a hat. But of course, he'd only intended to visit the roadside points of interest—the Long Logs trailhead, the scenic pull-outs, the old Studebaker marking the original Route 66. And he had sneered at the unreadiness of the hapless boy, who had probably never dealt in maps in his sheltered, electronic life.

The compass, though; Howard had brought a compass. Did that mean he'd had it in mind all along to take her away from the road and into the wildness? She let herself dwell on the thought as she plodded onward. After a while she caught herself humming, a little French tune that she had sung as a child.

The further they went, the more the heat enveloped her. It blew through her teeth and pressed into her lungs. A smell of searing purity—like hot stones or well-cured hay—arose and grew stronger. She stopped once and looked back toward the dunes. The boy was nowhere in the sweep of her vision. The air and land quivered with heat.

Howard had stopped walking. He stood, glowing red, without speaking.

"What is it?" He was always the slow one, but she was not expecting a full-out halt.

He was huffing perceptibly. "Let's sit down a moment. Rest." With that, he sank to his knees in the wash and quickly dropped back onto his buttocks.

She crouched beside him, feeling the fierce hotness that swarmed up from the sand, reluctant to sit for fear of burning. "You're alright? Drink a little." She offered her water bottle.

He held it high and gulped and gulped. He rubbed his hand over his lips and chin.

"I'm okay. Sure." Howard gave back the water bottle and rocked himself forward and up. "Have to move, though. I'm getting flambéed."

As he stepped forward—more slowly than before?—Clare kept herself next to him. She thought of taking his arm. Maybe later. The bluff held itself before them, a wall of shadow. The climb up would be steep. Again, she glanced behind her at the stark brilliance.

"We won't be quick. We'll just keep moving," said Howard. His breath still competed with an ambient desert hum as the most noticeable sound in her ears.

How coldly the day had begun, and now she had to walk beneath the sun-fire, in the beauty of pure incineration. Step after step, the wash utterly dry, glittering in an onslaught of light. She wished she had her kerchief back, to wipe the grit from her nose and cheeks.

Out ahead, the rim held its distance, its road and cars and scattered people invisible from where she stood. If anyone up there was looking down, she and Howard must be two crumbs, two specks that barely progressed.

She couldn't help thinking, only for an instant, of the boy who might still be waiting near the Onyx Bridge. Was he carrying any water? How would he withstand this sun? She couldn't bear that for herself, being stranded, lost and alone in the desert.

In a few hours, when the sun was gone, a freeze would descend on this very spot—a shuddering, stiffening cold not to be endured. The painted dunes would be frozen dust, leeched of color. There would be nothing animate except lizards, impassive in their cracks and holes—and the boy, if he was still out there.

Elizabeth Schoettle

LEN

Midnight. Three days since he gave me his phone number, but I haven't called him. Instead, I decided to make a piece of art and give it to him with my phone number on it, *The Scream*, this tiny Edward Munch post-card Edward bought for me at the Neue Gallery last year, the night of their grand opening. It's great. I pasted my character's pink head to *The Scream*'s head and on the back wrote my name and phone number. Then I put it inside a brown envelope, and since the envelope was brown and you would not be able to see black writing on the brown, I stuck mask-ing tape over it and wrote **LEN** in black on that; I marched out my door, no jacket required, the first hot, hot, day of spring, very beautiful... to deliver the card to the building where the stranger I'm crazy about lives.

The doors are automatic. Len (the stranger) lives in a building where doors slide. The lobby is dark, mahogany, I saw four elevators, a door-man's desk to the left, the air conditioning was on, and it was so cool it made me think of that hotel we stayed at in Bermuda when I was ten.

"Hi," I was dressed all in black; there was still glue on my hand from gluing (I've been making more artwork than ever, all about Len), "could you please give this to Len." I handed the doorman my card; he was short, old, typical.

I watched the doorman look down at the name... for a second I was nervous; did Len really live here, maybe Len was lying, he did say he lies..."I'm a social liar"... but then (hooray!) the doorman knew who Len was! "Thank you so much!" Automatic doors...

Hot sun going down... I took the park route to the gym, very pleased with myself, very pleased indeed, the entire walk there I replayed the note in my head: *The Scream*, not my creation of course, but good. It was original and unique, and Len would love me for it, I was sure. I wondered what he was doing at the time of my delivery; was he there, upstairs, was he masturbating? Or was he out getting bread? I ran into him on the street once carrying a bag of fancy fluffy bread and green lettuce that reminded me of Easter. I shop at the supermarket, I read the flyer, I buy multiple quantities of frozen beans on sale for eighty-eight cents. Yesterday I bought fourteen boxes. "Do you cook for yourself," he asked me that first night and I said, "Yes." But what would he say if I told him that I rip open the frozen vegetable boxes, (three), drop them into my red soup pot, then cut my onion as fast as humanly possible, put that in the red soup pot, cut my pepper, red soup pot, water chestnuts, pot, a whole bag of frozen spinach that gives me irreparable gas, pot, one pack of mushrooms, pot, then turn on the burner and let this stew for two hours until it's crust. Or maybe he was sitting on a park bench soaking up the heat, he's young, twenty-eight years old and he hates his mother. Later on, I'll find out he enjoys peppermint tea.

But forget all that!

Cut to home! And Len! Len was on my answering machine!

Wow, I put my bags down and listened, I was sick; this is how it starts, relationships, the first message on my answering machine from a much younger man, I would save this message forever (well it might be the only one he ever leaves. Truly, we may go out and he might hate me, but at least we would go out). Len told me in the message to call him if I wanted to take a break/distraction. (!!!!)

Oh, it felt just like the movies... I was in the shower, washing my hair. ... I was shaving my legs, scrubbing my face, thinking about Len (I love Len); I would call him when I got out of the shower and tell him 'Yes, we can meet.'

"... Gorgeous fuckin night," he had said (on my answering machine) about the night, oh, fuckin, the way he said fuckin... well: fuck me, is all I could think, and what am I going to wear? I was now drying off, staring at my phone. I had to call him back now and tell him I would, yes, like a distraction, I would like to do something in the gorgeous "fuckin" night.

*Though I can't remember if I dialed his number off the page, he wrote it on for me that day at the gym (of my book—I edit while I stretch because I hate coffee shops), if I rewrote it into my phone book, or if I replayed the message and memorized his number, then dialed... oh god, these details are important; they make a book work—did I do it while standing at my window in my towel? Or was I on my bed??
"Hi, Len?"

"Yes."

Oh my god! I could hear his TV on in the background; oh my god, it sounded like he was lying down in the dark, maybe holding onto his penis; I imagine he does that a lot.

"How are you?" I was looking at my legs in the mirror, they looked good I thought, strong and tan and, how are you, stupid, he hates that question (it's one of the first things he told me, never ask me how I am, because you really don't want to know the answer); I know, but I was nervous. This is someone I really like; I've never written about someone I really like; it's like picking up that instrument you always wanted to play.

"I'm watching *Fat Boy Run*," Len told me.

"Oh." I just stood there thinking about my hair. It was humid out; my hair would not perform well under such conditions.

"I've never seen it," I told Len, it was a stupid conversation. "Is that on cable?"

"Yeah," Len sounded bored, "so you wanna get out for a little while," he asked and YES, I was tan (I self-tanned yesterday thank god!), my hair was good (so far)... it was eight forty-five on a Sunday fuckin' gorgeous night, Edward didn't call me all day.

"Yes," I told Len, and Len sounded excited, he told me about this place he goes. "Yeah, fifteen minutes," I told him, along with my address; Len said he would meet me outside my door in fifteen minutes. And so, the next fifteen minutes were spent (you know) before my mirror obsessively trying to figure out how to make my hair **very perfect**—but it was not going to be perfect: this was evident. It was too humid, and I was too horny, staring at my face... wondering what it would be like to fuck Len.

We were walking fast up Sixth Avenue; the first warm night, he had on a white t-shirt with tightish sleeves, the kind I'm used to seeing him wear at the gym that accentuate his muscles, the ones I've always found embarrassingly macho and said I'd never date a guy who would wear sleeves like those.

"Oh really," we were crossing Sixth Avenue—(discussing tattoos), Len was leading—you can tell Len likes to be in control and fine, I was just following, I didn't mind, I enjoyed listening to him talk about himself, he likes to talk about himself, I don't of course understand half of what he's talking about because I'm too busy wondering what it would be like to rip his clothes off, throw him down and fuck him.

"So, if you ever got one," we crossed at the light and Len veered us left onto Greenwich, I'd forgotten already how tired I was, my jaw wasn't even hurting, but I had taken pain medication.

"What would you get," I asked him, I was looking at his shoes (Len walks faster than me and the sidewalks were crooked, I had to pay attention) But his shoes! Of course! His shoes are the first thing I looked at when we greeted each other to see if they were the cowboy boots with the sharp toenail tip I saw him come into the gym several times wearing—this is before Len and I had spoken a word to one another; we just passed each other with telepathic fuck eyes, six months of torture that made me ask every person I know if I should consider a man who would wear sharp-tipped snakeskin cowboy boots that curl up like a ski, and they all said absolutely not: any man who wears cowboy boots is either gay or he hates his mother. But much to my delight his shoes tonight were beautiful: rich, beige, flat, quite European and worn. They had small laces that were tightly tied, his body looked extra lean, he reminded me very much of my old boyfriend from college, Joe, the one who I did love but unfortunately crushed like a car, because the eating disorder won out, hurrah! Bulimia. Another relationship I lied in.

"END," we cut diagonally across Seventh Avenue to Waverly.

"END?" I looked at LEN.

"Yeah." I loved watching his mouth move in the dark; the trees were twisted, thin and haunted, I thought they looked like my hair. My hair felt huge, was my face too shiny, what color were my eyes in the dark? I can't recall what Len and I were talking about before crossing Hudson, just that we were walking close enough to be holding hands, but we were not. We were approaching a large restaurant on the corner of some unfamiliar street, with black awnings that seemed to zoom in. I wanted to tell Len I was sorry if things appeared clumsy or there was this *too* fresh look in my eye like someone had placed me in a garden for the first time... only because, "Thank you," the door was glass, Len held the door—there was a ramp (we were here)... a restaurant, what I pass every night and go to all the time, *and* I'm a waitress (what was my problem), a place where people laugh, talk, dine, and drink, and yet it suddenly felt like I'd never seen one.

"Isn't this nice," Len said about the restaurant, and I said, "Yes."

There were a lot of women in the room (big and low-lit), all pretty wearing makeup, sling-back dresses and high shoes that clicked past Len while we stood at the hostess desk waiting. I did not have on makeup, skin-revealing clothing or shoes that click. I had on my green army pants (that used to fall off my hips but now fit), this cream-colored t-shirt that said something about the invention of the light bulb in small brown cursive letters. I carried an oatmeal-colored cashmere sweater through my elbow. I was casual and lost. And yet I told myself relax, you've been cooped up under some old man's bed for ten years, breathe Phoebe.

"Do you have a table outside," Len asked the pretty young hostess, the place was packed, but she said yes, "It'll take just one moment," because Len was charming to the hostess. Then Len asked me if I liked sitting outside. "Yes," I told him. I hate sitting outside, I never sit outside, I don't know what it's like to sit outside—whenever Edward asks me if I want to sit outside, I say no.

We were led through the noisy crammed (for a Sunday night) room to a tiny outdoor table I would never in a million years sit at. "Thank you, perfect," I smiled at our hostess, took my tiny metal seat. Menus were placed before us: paper, lightweight, mine blew out of my hand immediately and hit Len in the face, I apologized.

"No problem—" Len handed it back. (God.)

"Thank you." I recall staring at the gray cement over the canvas railing that separates the restaurant from the public sidewalk thinking I might fall down and die right there, the night would be over, the ambulance would come, and Len would be shaking his head while they loaded me onto the stretcher, asking himself how these types always find him.

"I had the swordfish last time—" I watched Len repositioning his chair the way one does at the pool. (On our walk over we spoke about swimming, that's right, I asked him if he knew how to swim, and he looked at me like I was crazy. "Since I was born," he told me, and I thought oh, that's a good sign, I don't trust people who don't know how to swim.)

"Oh really?" I too was now looking at the menu (or trying to, crazy what the feeling of love does to a person). A man delivered water to us, bread, but I wasn't thinking about bread, I was just thinking about how I was looking at a new menu with words on it I couldn't read, I mean I was looking at that menu twenty minutes and saw not one word aside from "swordfish" and not because I saw the word but because Len said they have it. My jaw was shaking—God, I could not make it stop shaking (as hard as I tried). I even put my elbow on the table and discreetly held my jaw. Len kept smiling and talking. But I wonder if he noticed my shaking. Len offered me some bread— "Thank you."

I wanted to ask him what his favorite color was, what his favorite foods are. "Do you have an all-time favorite movie?"

"*Ghostbusters*," Len laughed. "Yeah," he reached for his water, "My mother took me when I was six and I ran out screaming."

"Oh really." I watched his eyes connected to his strong nose, his lips: red berry, I picked up a piece of bread. Even the way this man sits, he's like a building, so firm, so planted, so sure.

"Oh gosh Len, *The Muppets*, that's so funny." Your eyes are like ice on the lake in late December (even though it's early May) so cold so appealing, I wanted to leap over to your eye, put my skates on, climb in, and glide around and around.

"Did you want an appetizer?" Our waitress was fat and had on a bad jean skirt that Len and I both acknowledged as bad. Len says jean skirts are for twelve-year-olds and women who wear them are just trying to be young.

"No thank you," I told her. Len ordered one though, a salad of some sort that I didn't see on the menu, he said something about the "noki" here being the best he's ever had; I nodded and thought: what's noki, and now I have to eat. I wasn't even hungry. I ordered the swordfish but only because he told me to. The first night we spoke at the gym (the best night of my life, when he sat down under the black and white wall clock, put his hand out and said his name) Len told me that he was a bully, and when I asked him if it was physical, he said no, mental, but that 'mental is worse.'

I also had a Diet Coke. There were about five hundred servers and one of them asked if we wanted any 'real' drinks, I remember looking up at her; she was thin wearing blue, and she had short blond hair... Len was holding the wine list (the way Edward used to) asking if I wanted a glass, and when I said no, "I don't drink," he did this thing with his neck; yes Len's neck definitely inched forward, even the girl's neck taking the order moved.

"As in not ever," Len looked at me, he has no hair, or very shaved, but very handsome, and I said, "Yes, as in not ever."

"Well," he leaned a little further into his chair, "I'm ordering one."

"So, you really don't drink," Len said with a pitched eyebrow after his wine had arrived, and he was holding it in his hand like an old man wearing a bathrobe and slippers, dog by his side, and a fire roaring.

"No." I was trying not to fidget, to look like I did not want to have my legs wrapped around his face.

Len asked me what I do for relaxation, I did not have an answer to this question; others have asked me as well. I was chewing my bread listening to my jaw pop, worse than fucking ever. I remember wanting to tear his shirt off like wallpaper.

Then Len told me he was a photographer. "Oh wow." I reached for my Diet Coke and sat up straighter.

"Yeah," he had bread in his mouth, "but I'm still trying to figure it out..." He talked a lot with his hands and moved his head around too much.

A siren blew by, and an empty plate was delivered to me by a short dark-skinned man with a maroon tie and a white apron. Len stared at me, and I stared at him then down at the plate. Then the salad came, it was small and dressed. Len gazed at me, lifted the plate slightly, he wanted to give me some of his salad.

"Oh," I hesitated, and he took the plate that was in front of me, I watched him push salad off with his fork—and by the way, my napkin? I was mortified, because when I looked over at Len's side of the table, what did I see? No napkin. Len's napkin was on his lap (obviously) where it had been since he sat down and where was mine???? AAHHHHHHH- HHHHHHH!!!! ON THE TABLE UNDER MY FORK AND KNIFE!

I discreetly pulled the napkin from under my silverware. "Delicious, thank you."

Overdressed, I tasted cheese, parmesan, I hate cheese, he had the wine in his hand, clearly enjoying himself. I picked up my soda, wiped my mouth, I should also mention my lips—as a result of the acne medication I'm taking, that has a list of side effects ten miles long—were so dry I was getting mad at myself, at one point I even dragged my falling to pieces black bag onto my lap and started going through the garbage in search of the Blistex I would have given my right thumb to have found. I wonder if Len noticed how dry they were or that I kept needing to run my tongue over them to moisten them or that I was biting them, or that I wanted to bite his. Len has nice teeth, not affected by age, at 28, where was I at 28?

"So," Len sipped his wine, his second glass (that arrived sometime right after his first). "Do you know the difference between good food and bad food?"

"Oh?" I put down my fork, I felt lettuce in my teeth, horrible lettuce, like tree branches, and I told him, "Yes," but I don't actually, I just eat to eat . . . standing up in my tiny dark dusty disgusting kitchen with the one windowsill that will not stay clean (yesterday I stuck my hand through many cobwebs that grew back in five seconds). A few dogs went by, Len said to look at the way they were trotting, "like horses." Len talks a lot about dogs, he compares human beings to dogs constantly, also to other animals such as ants, birds—we spoke about birdcages and how young women in books are always being put into birdcages. I smiled and picked up my fork. I wanted to touch his leg under the table, but I didn't dare.

And then our dinners arrived. My swordfish, a small thick piece, "Thank you," with something underneath it, wet and green—Len looked up to make sure I was pleased, and I beamed, "Perfect." After that my side of asparagus came out, but very thin, the thinnest pieces of asparagus you ever saw, coated in oil. I'd have sent it back if I were out with Edward. Len had this huge *insurmountable* piece of chicken. "Here," he would say several times during the meal, "have some, there's about three chickens on my plate," and I distinctly recall it was—"Delicious—" during one of those times as I was reaching my fork and knife across the table to cut into his chicken, that felt so good to cut into (like we were dating!), I opened my BIG mouth and said to the man I have been dying to get alone for the past six (*excruciatingly*) long months, the words, "**I've never even had sex.**"

"Really," and he just sort of smiled this youthful grin, like what the fuck did she just say.

"Well," Len was incredibly disturbed at this information, and I was suddenly very sorry I'd said it. "You're thirty-four, you dated a man for ten years," he stabbed his chicken and ate it, "that's really fucked up, you know that don't you?"

Yes. Dark turn. I also mentioned (stupidly) we never slept in the same bed for the ten years we were together, wow I thought he was going to throw his plate onto the sidewalk, turn up the table, wipe his mouth and say, good luck to the man you meet in the future, glad I'm not him. I asked Len if "it's terrible," my not having had intercourse. And "No," he responds with a deep shoulder shrug, "but it's a tall order to fill." END OF.

"I just think that's really fucked up, and sad." Len waved his knife; he said Edward must have some serious issues to be with a woman that long who is clearly as unhappy as I was.

Tomorrow, four AM. We stayed out the whole night. After dinner we walked to the river where I remember telling Len, "I could have lied." But Len said, "No you couldn't." Then we went all the way to Soho, to a bar called Shade where we sat on barstools by candlelight. And no there may not have been a kiss, or air-conditioning for that matter, but we stayed out *seven* hours, that's the longest I've ever stayed out with any man.

I didn't even want to go to bed, I just wanted to wait until four o'clock in the afternoon when I'd get to see him at the gym. My apartment was dark and lonely (with clutter), and I remembered: dentist appointment, throbbing cheek, my six-hundred-dollar dental appointment at 2:45 on the Upper East Side. I stood at my black window holding the side of my face, my pain medication had worn off; the ache was back—"See you at the gym tomorrow, Len"—and it was hard to believe I was considering this, but Len goes to the gym at four... if the appointment overlapped ... well I had to see his face, if it would be happy to see me or if there would be disappointment in it. I called up my dentist at four-thirty in the morning, the dentist I'd been trying to get an appointment with all month and left a message to please cancel my appointment. I said I'd been up all night with some terrible flu.

Then I hung up, took a sleeping pill and when I got up the sun was out, almost noon, and I was back to thinking about Len.

I remember we passed a billboard on our way home that said: EMPTINESS IS ON YOUR SIDE.

Catherine Uroff

THE LAST SUPPER

They're only in Milan for a day, coming in late at night after a long
layover in London. At the hotel, Lauren gets to the front desk first,
quickly handing over her corporate AmEx card and passport to the
sleepy-eyed clerk.

"So, tomorrow," Richard says, patting his pockets to find his wallet.
"Looks like our morning is free. Meetings don't start until the afternoon,
that's what I'm trying to say. Maybe we could use that time to our ben-
efit. Explore a little. See the city."

"The two of us? Together?"

He watches her sign her registration card. She's careful about it. If
she was a kid at school, she'd have her elbows on the table, her head bent
low to the paper, a slip of her tongue snaking out of her mouth.

"Well, sure. I mean, why not? Right?"

He hurries to check in. She doesn't wait for him. At the elevators, she
pushes the up-arrow button even though it's already lit.

"I'm not sure what you've heard about me," Richard says, lowering
his voice even though there's no one else around. "But none of it is true.
Not a word."

This is the first time he's traveled with Lauren. She's a new hire, a recent MBA grad, brought into the department to help shape the corporate brand. Richard's boss, Davy, actually said those words when he
announced her arrival to the team, using his hands to carve something
in the air. But, clearly, and this is something he fumes about in his room
in Milan as he paces the narrow strip of floor between the king-sized bed
and the dressing table—even though he should be getting ready for bed,
he's dog tired, his ears are still plugged up, he can still feel the thrum of
the plane's engines coming in from the soles of his feet—she's already
heard about the meeting he had with Davy last month. At this point, it
seems as if everyone in the office knows about it. He can tell from the
way his co-workers pass him in the hallways, averting their eyes, turning
their bodies slightly to give him more room.

"Gotta talk to you about a sensitive issue," Davy said when he summoned him into his office, late on a Friday afternoon. "Well, to be honest here, Rich, it's more than just an issue. There've been some complaints."

"Like what?"

"It's a different world we live in now."

"Sure, it is. Don't have to tell me that one."

Richard was anxious to get back to his desk, organize his files, respond to one last email, water the spider plant that sat on top of the slim storage cabinet in his cubicle. His sister, Marilyn, was making him dinner that night and he needed to stop by the package store to pick up a bottle of wine.

"People take everything very seriously nowadays," Davy was saying, and Richard felt a roll of irritation, a short rumble in his gut as if he'd just eaten something rich. What was his boss talking about?

"Well, that's a good thing. Isn't it? I mean, you want your employees to take their jobs seriously."

"Yeah, no, I'm talking about something else. This is all off the record, by the way. For now. Nothing's official just yet, Richard, which should make you feel better."

"I feel fine. Why wouldn't I?"

"Here's the thing," Davy said and then he went on to describe the alarming talk that'd been going around lately among the female staff in the department. Apparently, there was the overall consensus that Richard treated his female colleagues in a manner that was deemed borderline inappropriate at best, if not downright harassment. He made women in the company uncomfortable with the way he spoke to them in an overly fond way, touched them while he was trying to make a point, showed no respect for their personal space.

"We have to have a zero tolerance for this kind of thing," Davy said.

"You can't believe this horseshit."

"I've been trying to hold them off. What with all you've been through with Jolie—." Richard held his hand up.

"Leave my wife out of it."

"Okay. No offense meant. I'm trying to help you here."

After a few more minutes, Richard excused himself. He thanked Davy for the feedback and said that he'd be more thoughtful and considerate towards others. When Davy reminded him that he really needed to straighten up, that everything was unofficial for now but he couldn't keep it that way if more complaints came in, he was proud of his restraint, pleased that he hadn't become outraged, hadn't reminded Davy of other transgressions in the office, like Arnold Molnar showing up drunk for work for four months straight after his dog died; Tom Sturgeon threatening the lives of his creditors who repeatedly called his office phone; Paul Jameson playing online solitaire on his computer for six hours every day.

He didn't even bring up Davy's own offenses, which were, in large part, why his marriage to Betty—a sweet woman who used to bake sugar cookies for their department to mark each holiday: ghosts for Halloween, turkeys for Thanksgiving, candy canes piped with red and white frosting for Christmas—had fallen apart. Like the time Davy got drunk at an after-hours party at their annual dealer show in Las Vegas, and made a pass at his admin, Denise. Everyone saw it: Davy and Denise, stumbling against each other as they headed, hand-in-hand, towards the elevator banks in the Bellagio's grand lobby. After that trip, Denise started coming in late every day and she refused to do the simplest of tasks—take meeting notes, schedule workshops, order lunch. But Davy couldn't fire her, couldn't even write her up, because of what had happened between them in Vegas. She was there for years until one day she just stopped coming in, and Davy asked Richard to box up the things on her desk and send them to her via USPS.

In Milan, Richard meets Lauren in the hotel's dining room for breakfast. She shows up wearing track pants and a t-shirt with a ripped collar. Her light brown hair is limp around her face. She says she isn't hungry. She sounds tired and something else. Defeated.

"You sure you don't want anything to eat?" he asks. "Today's going to be a long one." "I'm fine. Please. Go ahead," she says.

He goes up to the elaborate, multi-station breakfast buffet and gets an omelet from the chef behind the grill. When he comes back to their table, she's swiping her phone very quickly, shaking her head.

"So, what do you think? You and me, seeing the sights? I'm actually looking forward to it," he says after the waitress brings him a cappuccino with a little milk heart floating on top of it. "That is, if you're okay with it."

When she sighs, Richard readies himself for her response. She'll tell him that she doesn't want to go anywhere with him, that he's been presumptuous to assume she would. Or maybe she'll remind him that they are there for business only and what they really should do is find a quiet space somewhere in the hotel to go over the meeting agenda, to make sure they're "on the same page" in order to "move the needle." That's how she talks. Just the week before, he sat through one of her presentations about marketing funnels and how the company needed to start efficiently leveraging content to target niche audiences to ensure their customers were aligned with their strategic goals.

"I want to see the *Last Supper*," she says instead.

"What now?"

"The mural painted by Leonardo da Vinci. It's here, in Milan."

"Oh, yes. That one. Sure."

"Leonardo painted it on a wall in a church in downtown Milan. My mother saw it once, years ago, when she was my age. I've always wanted to see it and now's as good a time as any. But really, you shouldn't feel like you need to join me. This is my thing. Not yours. You're not obligated or anything like that."

"Nonsense. It sounds like a lovely idea. I love it. I'm only sorry I didn't think of it sooner. I'll go anywhere you'd like. Honestly. Your wish is my command."

She pauses.

"Don't."

"Don't what?"

She doesn't answer. She just looks down at her phone. He finishes his omelet and as soon as he's done, she pushes back from the table and stands up.

Back in his room, Richard takes time to brush and floss his teeth, gargling with the mini bottle of mouthwash that is branded with the hotel logo. Then he changes into a polo shirt that Marilyn gave him for his last birthday. When he gets down to the lobby, Lauren is already there, still wearing the same rumpled workout clothes that she wore at breakfast. It doesn't even look as if she's combed her hair. If she was anyone else— Brad DiMarco from Support, a good guy if a little boring, always going on about his latest rescue dog, or Michael Chasen from Sales, who liked to brag about his pilot's license—Richard would tease her for looking the way she does, for sticking out among the other smart-looking people swarming around them, businessmen in slim-fitting suits, checking their watches, talking on their phones.

Outside, the sun sparkles against the blank windows of the skyscrapers across the street. They walk under an overpass, follow some trolley tracks, and then cross into an older neighborhood that has windy cobblestone streets, elegant apartment buildings painted in pretty hues of pink and yellow, flower shops with sunflowers and hydrangeas and daisies in tin boxes outside their doors. Lauren walks quickly, keeping her head down, barely waiting at the curb for the light to change. Richard takes care not to get too close to her, not to swing his arms and touch her. According to Davy, that's one of the objections that the women at work have. Apparently, when Richard walks down the hall, he veers too close to them, brushes their arms. Some of the women don't think it's done accidentally either.

"You're a close talker too," Davy said during their meeting, explaining that there was a woman in Accounting who didn't like the way Richard got nose-to-nose with her whenever they spoke. Richard figures that complaint must've come from Melanie Ingersall, a young woman who kicks back his expense reports for the most trivial reasons: miscategorizing a $22 expense, missing a receipt for an $11 breakfast, being $3 off of the company per diem allowance.

Whenever Richard receives the automated email notification—*Your Expense Report has been denied. Please correct and resubmit*—he goes down to the 2nd floor, finds Melanie in her cubicle, tries to jolly her into approving his expenses. He offers her a piece of gum, asks about her family, chats about her vacation plans, compliments her latest hairstyle. Melanie always laughs, shooing him away. "Okay, fine, Richard, you win," she says. Now she's complaining about him, too.

"Oh no," Lauren says. "Goddammit no."

She stops so suddenly that he almost bumps into her. Behind the church, in front of the convent, there's a long line of people in front of the ticket booth, other tourists laughing and chatting together.

It's the first time he's heard her express any kind of emotion. At Heathrow, when their hours-long flight delay to Milan was announced, she didn't even flinch. She just opened up her company laptop, balanced it on her knees, and started typing. Now she has her hand over her mouth.

"It's okay. The line will go fast, I'm sure," he says.

"We don't have a lot of time this morning."

"We have all the time in the world. Trust me. We'll see this painting. Come hell or high water. You ever heard that expression? People don't use it that often these days but that's how I feel. Come hell or high water, we'll see what you want to see. We'll have a lovely morning together just looking at art. How about that?"

He's grinning so widely that his cheeks hurt. She drops her hand from her face. She looks like she always does. Stone face, that's what he thinks of it. Dead eyes. Closed lips. There's not a trace of anything on her face. No lines. No color. No movement. She doesn't even blink.

It takes thirty minutes to get to the top of the line. The lady behind the desk shakes her head at them. The tickets are sold out. Nothing available for the morning. If they really wanted to see the *Last Supper*? They should've bought tickets in advance, like everyone else. Online.

Lauren swears again. This time, she puts her hands up to her head like she's nursing a headache.

"I can't believe it. I'm this close and I can't see it," she says. "Fuck me."

"Next time," the ticket taker says.

"There is no next time," Lauren snaps.

"We're flying out tonight," Richard says.

"All sold out now. Next time. Buy tickets online."

"Signora, can't you please help us out? Per favore? This young lady, well, she really wants to see the *Last Supper*. Grazie. Grazie mille," Richard says, using the few Italian words he knows.

The ticket taker looks like a stern grandmother in her dark, long-sleeved dress, thick white hair put up in a bun, glasses hanging from a thin cord around her lined neck, hawkish nose, thin lips. Still, he thinks it might work. She'll slip them a few tickets. She'll feel Lauren's wretchedness and be charmed by his smile and make an exception. What are two more tickets anyway?

"All sold out now. Maybe next time," she repeats.

Compared to the crowd outside, the church is relatively empty, just a few tourists milling about the aisles, murmuring to each other as they look up at the adorned domed ceiling, the carved pillars, the embellished arches. Richard finds Lauren standing in front of a frescoed chapel, next to a table of yellow votive candles.

"Hey," he says, trying to sound hearty like he does during weekly staff meetings when he has to admit that sales are trending down this quarter and last. "This place is certainly beautiful. So, there's that. There's always an upside, right?"

"It's just a church. They all look pretty much the same."

He wants to disagree with her, describe the worship space on the fourth floor of Dana Farber's Memorial Wing, a dimly lit room with a stack of Bibles on a cart by the door. He went there every time Jolie was admitted to the hospital, a welcome escape from the busy corridors, incessant noises: the irregular beeps of the medical machines, the buzzing telephones, the overhead pages for doctors, snippets of cheerless conversations. Jolie had been brave about her cancer first, never crying when she lost her hair, when she shed fifteen pounds in a week and a half, when her white blood cell count got so low that she needed a transfusion. But two years into it, she'd had enough. "No more, Richie," she'd told him during her last hospital visit, as the nurse hooked her up to an IV. "I'm done." And once she'd made up her mind, she didn't waver, not once, not even when he begged her to stay the course, not even when he got so weak and pitiful that he got down on his knees to plead, to blubber that he couldn't live without her.

"You'll see the *Last Supper* another time. I'm sure of it," he says to Lauren now.

"You don't understand."

"I'm disappointed too. Believe me. To get this close to seeing something by the greatest artist in the world that ever lived. Wow. I feel cheated. I'll let you in on a little secret. I've never even seen the *Mona Lisa*. Wouldn't that be something? If I ever get to Paris, it's the first thing I'll do. Stand in front of the *Mona Lisa* and stare at it for hours."

"It's dark and under thick glass and you'll get about fifteen seconds to see it if you're lucky enough to battle through the crowd around you."

She pushes her hair away from her face. Richard can see her strained neck, her pale cheeks, the white outline of her lips.

"Lauren?"

There's something wrong with the way she's staring straight ahead. She looks like she's focused on something that's puzzling her but there's nothing in particular to look at, just a small, empty chapel with a simple altar set up on a wooden platform, a small gold cross surrounded by wrought-iron candelabras.

"Here," Richard says, "you'd better sit down."

He cups her elbow with his hand, leads her to a row of fold-up chairs inside the chapel.

"I'm fine," she says after she sits down.

"Of course, you are."

He sits next to her. It feels good to get off his feet. "I'll be fine for the meeting this afternoon."

"I have no doubt. You should've had something for breakfast, that's all."

"I shouldn't have come all the way here without tickets. It was a stupid idea. And look, having you go with me? It was just a waste of time."

"Nonsense. I enjoyed the walk."

"I need to be alone right now."

"I can't leave you when you're in this state. I'd worry too much."

She stares at him for a second. He feels like he has to sit up taller, suck in his gut. "People say things about you at work."

"Lies. All lies."

"This job is important to me. My career . . . well . . . I plan on going places."

"And you will. Nothing will stop you. Certainly not me. Hey, I was married and I never once, not once . . ."

After the dealer show in Vegas was over, he had run into Davy's admin, Denise, at the airport. She was standing in front of a row of slot machines, staring at the groggy travelers who were trying their luck one last time. He walked her to her gate, and she started to cry about some man who was no good, who was sure to break her heart. He knew she was talking about Davy, but he didn't let on. He went to the men's room to get her some paper towels so that she could wipe her eyes. Her tears brightened her face, and in the early morning staleness of that airport, with the rushing rings from the slot machines and the electronically voiced announcement of a recent gate change, a strange, small desire came up inside him, and he knew that if he suggested that they take a later flight back, that they go somewhere together nearby to talk some more, she would have agreed to it. But—and he thought this was something to be proud of—that wasn't what happened. As soon as Denise stopped crying, he left her, going to his gate where he took out his laptop and answered some work emails.

"I don't need to know all that," Lauren says.

"I'm just saying—I'm one of the good guys. Swear it, I am," Richard says. "And I think this was a swell idea. Seeing a masterpiece like the *Last Supper*. Just because it didn't work out doesn't mean that it wasn't a great idea."

"My mom and me? We were always going to see it together."

"And you still can. What'd I tell you? It'll be here . . . when you come back. It's not going anywhere, that's for sure."

She slumps forward, puts her elbows on her knees. He can see the delicate curve of her neck and thinks of Jolie, the way her thick, dark hair fell down to the small of her back. He suddenly wishes he could tell Lauren about her. She was the most vivacious person he'd ever known. She was a gourmet cook trained at Le Cordon Bleu. She made friends wherever she went, and everyone loved to make her laugh, to hear that rich sound bubbling out of her wide mouth.

"My mom got me tickets to Italy once. For my college graduation. It was supposed to be a trip around the world. Italy wasn't the only place. We were going to go all the way to Australia. See all there was to see. But I canceled at the last second."

"I'm sure you had a good reason why."

"I didn't. I was silly, thoughtless. I was having a tough time with my boyfriend and didn't want to be separated from him. I wanted to work on our relationship. So stupid. My mom was kind about it even though she'd put a lot of money down, even though I was her only child, she wasn't married, this was it for her. She said that she understood. She said that I had to take care of myself and do what was right for me. 'Don't worry about it,' she said to me. 'There'll be other trips.' Just like what you're saying. She was wrong though. There were no other trips. That was my one chance with her, and I blew it. She died a year later. We never went anywhere."

A woman with a bulging fanny pack strapped around her waist takes a few steps into the chapel. She bows her head when she sees them, slips into the pew in front of them, uses the padded kneeler to pray for a second, and then pops up again and leaves.

"I'm sorry to hear that. Damnit, I am."

"That boyfriend that I was so worried about? We broke up a month after her funeral."

"That's no good."

"Maybe I don't even blame him. It was too much for him. All my sadness and guilt."

"Carrying that around though. That's not right either."

He hopes she'll tell him more. Maybe he can tell her a sad story of his own, like how he always stayed in the hospital's makeshift chapel for far too long, desperate to postpone his return to Jolie's hospital room. "Where the hell have you been?" Marilyn would hiss every time he came back to the room because she was the one who was faithfully taking care of his wife, holding her limp and swollen hand, readjusting the scarf that had slipped off her bald head, checking for new bed sores, rubbing her slack arms with lavender-scented lotion, dampening her chapped lips with a small pink sponge. He didn't even do what he was good at: charming the nurses, cajoling them to find an extra pillow, adjust the bed, bring in a cup of ice chips.

"I thought that if I saw the *Last Supper*, my mother would somehow know about it. And she'd be happy. When she saw it, it was really bad. Barely visible on the wall. Like a ghost. All because Leonardo used the wrong kind of paint on the wall, or something like that. He was in a hurry, didn't want to take the time to do it properly. They've restored it now. Made everything clear. Brighter too. Who knows how much is left of the original painting though. But if they hadn't done it, it would've faded away to nothing. There would've been nothing left to see."

"Painted over it, did they?"

She laughs a little.

"Doubt they'd think of it that way."

"Listen, your mother? She'd want you to be happy. She wouldn't want you beating yourself up over things."

"I know."

"But it's tough. What you've gone through. Don't I know about it? My wife died. My Jolie. And I wasn't myself for a very long time. Maybe I was like that painting. Just disappearing. Little by little. Nothing left of me."

"Well, you don't have to—"

There's a warning in her voice that he tries not to notice.

"I just couldn't just bear up like everyone expected me to. Everyone expects you to grieve, yes, but there always comes a time when you're supposed to move on. And I couldn't. Not for a very long time. So, what I'm trying to say to you is . . . I imagine your mother was very lovely, if she was anything like you, and I bet you were a great daughter to her, a first rate one actually, and it's okay to be sad and feel like you lost something and it's okay to come all the way over here to see something and kinda fall apart when you can't but I'm here for you, honest, I am, and we'll stay right here all morning if we have to, and we can talk about your mother some more, if you want, or we can talk about something else entirely but the thing is, we'll be right here and we'll figure this out together."

He pauses and then puts his hand on the center of her back, right underneath her shoulder blades. He can feel the hard outline of her bra's band and inches his fingers above it. He pats her first, like a father consoling his child, and then his touch morphs into a rub, his fingers splayed out slightly and pressing lightly across the expanse of her back. Up and down and sideways, he covers more and more space as he tries to talk about a painting he's never seen, a woman he's never met.

"Get off me."

Lauren doesn't stiffen or jump up or even lean away from him. She just sounds disgusted, world-weary, and it's enough. Richard lets his hand drop. His leg is pressed against hers and he shifts in his seat, away from her, too.

"Now wait a minute."

"Who do you think you are?"

"We're having a good conversation."

"I didn't want you to do that."

"There's a misunderstanding here."

"You can't just go around touching people."

"Okay, okay, I hear you loud and clear."

"Creepy old man."

His lips tremble.

"Don't call names now. Please."

She swipes at her mouth with the back of her hand as if she's trying to rub away a kiss. "You'd better leave me alone."

"My wife—."

"I don't want to hear about her. I shouldn't have gone on about my mother. I wasn't thinking straight. It's being here... it got me thinking things. Messed me up. But you shouldn't have taken advantage of it."

"You're making me sound—."

"Everyone warned me about you."

"It's not true though."

"What's not true, Richard?"

It's the first time she's called him by his name. She's looking directly at him. The color has returned to her face.

"Go, please. Leave me alone," she says before he can answer. Richard gets up then and looks down at her.

"I'll wait for you outside," he says and when she doesn't respond, he walks out of the chapel. He turns back to look at her once, and she's kneeling. Her forehead rests on her folded hands.

He knows he should leave, head back to the hotel. If he wants to keep his job, he should call Davy, be the first to explain the situation and present his side of the story, insist that Lauren got upset and he'd been trying to console her. Certainly not an example of gross misconduct. She'd misunderstood his intentions. She seemed a little overwrought if he has to be honest. Then he'll change into his finest suit, call a taxi to deliver him to the Milan office early where he'll greet Italian colleagues. *Buon pomeriggio. Come va?* He'll explain that Lauren will be joining them shortly and that they both are very much looking forward to this visit.

Instead, he walks out of the church, into the bright sunshine gardens of the small, key-shaped courtyard at the back of the church and sits down on a bench by a neatly trimmed shrub. He doesn't move, even as the morning sun rises higher, burns hotter. Sometimes he mistakes another tourist for Lauren, half-rising from his seat, holding up his hand, calling out her name. But after a while all the young women begin to look alike to him—vibrantly or sullenly alive, it's all the same. They're beautiful, not like Jolie who was twisted up at the end, her disease's ugliness having spread from the inside out, shrinking the flesh from her bones, tunneling out her eyes, her loose, dark hole of a mouth.

He crosses his arms against his chest and leans back on the bench so that his legs stretch out on the path before him. He stops looking for Lauren, waiting for her to come out. He thinks maybe she's left already, found another exit, and he has to hand it to her. She's a strong woman, that's what he thinks, and he wishes he could tell her that even as he realizes that that's impossible now. He stays in the garden for a long time, thoughts of his wife and his colleagues and his cowardice slowly slipping away, until there's nothing left to think about but the *Last Supper*. He imagines that he's standing before it, that great piece of art designed to disintegrate. In his mind, the mural looks the way it used to, the way the artist left it—dim on a cracked wall. He strains to detect what's really there, and—after a while—he's able to catch glimpses of certain things: a curve of a foot, the outline of a table leg, the rippled folds of a robe.

Sarah Martin

MAGIC BIRTHDAY

Wasim woke me before my alarm went off.

"Good morning, happy birthday, but you need to leave now please!"

"Jesus, Wasim, it's not even five." The room was dark, and I couldn't find my bra anywhere.

"You don't need it anyway," said Wasim.

There was a small mountain of shoes near the front door, mine were easy to find as they were smaller than the others and the only white sneakers in the stack. Before I had a chance to put them on, Wasim had opened the door, gently pushed me out and handed me my backpack.

"My god, you said you weren't worried about me staying over last night."

"Whose god?" Wasim thought this was funny.

"You know I don't care, it can be your god today."

"Get out of here and text me later."

I searched my backpack for my scarf which I use to cover my head in Wasim's neighborhood. My god, his god, whatever—Istanbul is the most fantastic city in the world. I had saved two years to spend the entire month of May by myself in Turkey. Today was my thirty-fifth birthday, although I did not correct Wasim when he guessed it was my twenty-seventh.

The Gold Horn Bridge saw that I was making my way to her, and she began to sparkle as the sun rose. The minarets all stood at attention, they could not contain themselves, they erupted in song. The gulls had been learning a choreographed routine where they dove into the water and back to the bridge in unison, wings and waves filled the foreground, Hagai Sophia stood gloriously and triumphantly in the back, strong as any mountain.

Boys were learning to fish from the bridge with their grandfathers, while streetwise dogs snuck smelly treats from bait buckets. I had a standing invitation to visit my favorite bookstore on Istiklal Street. The last time I was at the store, a map revealed that it held a secret for me, but I had to come back on my thirty-fifth birthday to receive the details.

I'd learned to trust books and maps from a young age and was happy to return. On any other day, I would have been allergic to the dust and the cats that slept on every surface, but today I was immune.

The bells jingled behind me as I entered the shop. The building had once belonged to the Dutch embassy, but in the mid-1900's it had been purchased and turned into a bookshop which specialized in maritime history and antique maps. Once you set foot into the shop and began to take in the beauty, you couldn't help but gasp. Even for a sensible adult, while inside the shop, it felt easy to believe in magic, or love, or adventures. Painted whirling dervish dancers curtsied to me as I returned a "Hello, it's good to see you again."

Most of the antique maps were housed on the second floor, each step of the curved wooden staircase was littered with brass bells, wheels, lanterns, and salvaged parts of ships. My map was hanging exactly where I had left her two years before. Where now, dear map? I closed my eyes and pointed, when I saw where my finger had traveled it was to a location north of the city a few blocks west of the Bosphorus. I thanked the map and decided to spend my day walking to the address.

The noon prayer and my stomach were in sync. I saw a juice shop with hot pink, lilac, yellow, and blue chairs arranged on the patio and decided to order and watch young women, some with their mothers, others with their iPhones, wait in line for lunch. A favorite pastime had become jotting down t-shirt slogans that didn't quite translate the way intended from English to Turkish (or vice versa). Some of my favorite phrases were: *Girls just want to have dance, I am not a nugget, Play with your hair* and my favorite, *Your shape destroys you.*

I'd met Wasim a few days after my arrival in Istanbul in the tram station closest to Taksim Square. We both were attempting to buy a ticket, but the machine was broken and there was no attendant on duty. After we discovered we both spoke English, we laughed and decided to take a walk. We soon realized our smiles were broken in the exact same place. "How did you break your front tooth?" Wasim asked, laughing.

"I wish I could make up an interesting story, but the truth is I broke it on a beer bottle."

Wasim had chipped his front tooth back in Syria. Before he had left Syria, his best friend had been shot and immediately died in front of him. He and some other family members took refuge in Turkey and were working odd jobs to pay for a shared house. Wasim's English was impeccable, he was hoping to begin tutoring kids after school. Like most Muslims, Wasim did not drink alcohol, being with him was like being on a vacation from myself.

The Rumeli Fortress was the only landmark close to my destination. I climbed the hill and sat on top of the highest watchtower listening as a tour guide below recited facts about the Ottoman empire. The tourists took photos of the fortress and the boats bobbing along on the Bosphorus below. The mid-afternoon call to prayer echoed through the fortress, some of the tourists prayed in the small mosque housed inside the walls.

The address the map had shown me was gated and locked. When young children with backpacks rushed from the alley and opened the latch to the home, I followed. The garden boasted koi ponds, peacocks, and a sleepy old dog. The children gathered in the shade of the cypress trees, baby turtles had hatched, and they were gleefully choosing their names. An elderly woman joined the group with a bowl of cherries and apples. I watched as the children fed fruit to the adult turtles, twins in matching dresses painted likenesses of their tiny new friends on a large sheet of watercolor paper. One twin said, "Let's throw them their first birthday party!"

The woman looked at me and said something in Turkish. She motioned for us to follow her into the house. A small boy reached for me to hold him, I picked up the strange child and joined the others. The sunroom had been organized as an art room, short tables and tiny chairs held wiggly five-year-olds, spools of yarn and cups of paint.

The woman walked over to the piano and tapped one key. The children silently beamed, waiting for her announcement. Like an airplane attendant, the woman spoke first in Turkish, followed by Danish and then finally in English, "We shall celebrate with cake and balloons!" She dispensed marbled cake to the children, who were using their best manners to earn the largest slice. The boy was sitting on my lap, raising his tiny hand so she wouldn't overlook him. It occurred to me that the woman must have thought I was a new nanny. She gave the boy a slice of cake with gooey frosting and handed me a bag of deflated balloons.

As the party ate cake, I dutifully and happily filled the balloons with all the air I had in my thirty-five-year-old body. I took a marker and drew an animal face on each balloon while the children gathered around me. Before long, I had emptied the bag and we decided to march through the garden with our animal balloons to celebrate the baby turtles. The twins sang a song and waved streamers, conducting our parade. Parents arrived to gather their children as the sunset prayer rang through the neighborhood. I waved goodbye to the twins, the turtles, and to the woman who never asked who I was or what I was doing in her home.

Wasim texted and asked me to meet him at Taksim Square after Isha, the final call to prayer. I took a taxi to the square where Wasim was waiting, he had planned a surprise for my birthday. I followed him down the side streets of Istakal to a gymnasium. All the lights were on, and the sounds of laughter could be heard from the street. Wasim had me wait on the sidewalk as he made a phone call, speaking in Arabic.

Moments later, a young woman rushed to greet us from the gym and ushered us inside. The sounds of laughter had hushed, we sat in the empty stands facing the gym's center. The young woman blew a whistle and a group of teenagers emerged from the shadows spinning plates and dancing to the beat of Turkish dance music. Five girls in gold costumes entered on stilts where they somehow managed to gracefully move amongst the twirling. Wasim was pleased with my delight and told me that the students were part of a social circus school. Syrian and Turkish teenagers gathered and performed shows for young refugee children who had recently moved to Turkey and were struggling with adjusting to their new life.

After giving a standing ovation, I repeated the one Arabic phrase I knew for gratitude to Wasim, the teenagers, the map, the turtles, the sea: *Betshakkarak, Betshakkarak, Betshakkarak.*

David Wilde

THE RED OLEANDER

I live with the bomb every day. I live on the edge of a concrete platform peering down at train tracks. At times I want the courage to leap in front of that train.

I'm afraid to close my eyes. Time pulls me back like a strong current. Old, fragmented memories are like shattered windows. Emotions gather like schools of fish. I can't even say her name out loud.

Everything brings me back to that precipice, to that choice I made. Even now, sitting in my garden, sixty years later, old, wrinkled hands thrust deep inside the earth's soil. A blooming oleander flower brings me back to Hiroshima.

They said it would take one hundred years for the vegetation to return. But I saw it there, in the black scorched earth, beyond the train tracks. Its red petals were like a bright ruby in a dark room.

I was just a nine-year-old girl when the bomb dropped. My sister and I heard the airplane and ran to the low window. She was two years my junior. The propellers were loud and high above. A single black dot fell below. Everything flashed white, like an overexposed photograph. The ground roared and billowed. A tall pillar of ember lifted halfway to heaven.

We flew through the air.

I remember waking up. It felt like I was inside an oven. The skin on my arms and shoulders burned. My sister was screaming. I pulled her out of the rubble. The hot stones burned my hands. She cried out for mother.

I ran out into the backyard where Mother was hanging laundry. There was nothing left but an ocean of fire. A grey dust danced inside a strange wind. People wailed off in the distance.

I noticed a dark ashed figure kneeling down. It had black holes for eyes. I knew it was Mother because of her gold tooth. I reached out and touched her shoulder. Her burnt hollowed figure crumbled, then dissipated into the surrounding wind. She spread across the land like dandelion seeds caught in a gust.

I shut my eyes and cried.

I remember holding my sister's hand in the streets, yelling out for Father. The earth was black and scorched. Dead bodies were singed like grilled fish: skin shredded and falling off. Many had missing limbs and dark charcoaled faces: noses and ears wiped clean away. Others cried out for water, then fell over silent. They dropped like leaves from a tree.

We threw ourselves into the river, avoiding the heat. I was terrified, then became numb. A black rain fell, covering everything in a slimy mush.

And later, at the clinic, getting our burns treated. Bodies were wrapped in bleeding bandages. A man lay face down next to me. His entire backside was burned. And the flies, oh the hundreds of flies, buzzing and landing on our wounds. I heard the same man cry out to the nurse, "Kill me! Please kill me! I can feel the maggots eating my flesh."

Then the sickness came. They called it "Atomic Bomb Disease." We became lethargic and diseased: purple dots sprouted all over our bodies, clumps of hair fell out, our gums bleed and our organs swelled. They thought it was contagious. We were called the Pikadon People and treated like outcasts.

We built a simple shelter out of burnt wood and crumbled bricks. There was no food. We were always hungry. The only things we didn't eat were the mice and dogs. We couldn't catch the mice; they were too fast. We stayed away from the dogs; they were too mean. We mostly stole burnt corn and stale rice. It was about this time that my sister stopped talking. She only quietly whispered for Mother while sleeping.

Then the Americans came with their jeeps. The doctors studied our sickness but didn't treat it.

"Hallo! hallo (hello)!" I'd shout to the soldiers, the only American word I knew. They'd give us canned meats and bread. I hated them, and I hated us.

My sister and I were at the train station one day, looking for food. She was despondent now: face of stone, eyes drifting around like lazy clouds.

I saw some GI's walking on the platform and ran towards them, leaving my sister by the tracks. I was consumed by grief. "Give Mother back to me!" I shouted, "give her back!" The GI's just smiled, not understanding my words. One of them gave me a stick of gum.

I turned to see my sister, standing on the edge of the concrete platform. She was looking to her left at the oncoming train. I called her name.

She looked back and smiled over her shoulder.

I'll never forget that look. Her face hangs like a painting in my house. I study its crevices and bends, trying to unlock its secrets. There was a hint of love hidden in her barren cheeks. She jumped and was forever lost to me. She never even got to try chocolate.

I found myself standing at the same spot a week later. I wanted to be with mother. I looked to the left for the train. The ground started to rumble. I felt the train's strength in my feet. The steel machine turned the bend. It coughed grey smoke into a blue sky.

I thought I heard somebody call my name. I looked back over my shoulder at an empty platform. I smiled to no one. The train whistled. I turned back and tiptoed closer to the edge. I looked down and saw the rocks around the steel rods vibrating.

It takes courage to die.

I glared out into the vast burnt field across the tracks, noticing a speck of color. It radiated like a bright star. I focused my eyes and noticed a small oleander flower blooming in the darkness. Its green stem burrowed through the dark ash. Delicate red petals reached up for the sun.

It takes courage to live.

I fell back onto the hard concrete as the train whooshed by. My eyes watered and my hair swirled.

Old burns are birthmarks now. Here, sitting in my garden, the red flower brings me back. I chose, I often remind myself. I had a choice, and I chose. I continued to choose through the sickness, the leukemia, and a miscarriage.

Sweat gathers on my brow as I water the dark soil. I think of my daughter, recently married. There will be a child soon. I know the bomb is deep inside: dead cells, broken bonds, mutated DNA. I worry that I'll

pass the bomb on. That my daughter's child will be born un-whole.
I live with the bomb every day.

Bob Chikos

2019 FORT DEARBORN STATE UNIVERSITY COMMENCEMENT ADDRESS

The floor of the basketball arena is filled with row upon row of black polyester robe-clad soon-to-be graduates. In the stands sit family members, holding plastic-wrapped flowers and homemade signs as the young ones squirm uncomfortably. On the stage are administrators of importance, wearing cloth robes, and repeatedly checking their watches.

From the side of the stage walks a man, about seventy, with white hair, aviator glasses, and the black polyester robe of an undergraduate. He is announced as "Commencement Speaker Steve Chicanetti, the oldest member of the December 2019 graduating class of Fort Dearborn State University."

"You're probably wondering 'Who is this old guy? And why is he delivering the student address?' First, I need to tell you a little about me. When I graduated from high school, back in nineteen *cough-cough*, I had a choice: I could pay money to go to college, or I could start working right away and get paid. At the time it seemed like a real no-brainer.

"I had a forty six-year career, all on a factory floor. Every day for forty six years, my alarm woke me up at four a.m. for my shift. On my last day, I put that alarm clock into a press and smashed it into a million pieces!

"I can't tell you how many times I wished I'd-a went to college. I'd be doing the same thing, day after day, week after week, month after . . . well, you get the idea. And I'd wonder how my life would have been different had I gone to college. Maybe I would've gotten into management. Maybe I would've done something with my mind.

"Many times, I'd be in a social situation, and someone'd say, 'So, where did you go to college?' I'd say, 'I never went to college' and they'd have an embarrassed look like they pointed out a handicap or something. But in a way, they'd have been right. It has been a handicap.

"I have two sons. You better believe they went to college. Best investment I ever made. I was happy for them, but also a bit jealous. I always wondered, 'What if?'

"When you retire, you don't *have to* do anything. You can sleep 'til noon and spend all day in your pajamas. I know I did a few times. And I wondered, *Is this all there is to life?* I thought about all the things I always wanted to do. At the top of my list was college.

"I talked it over with my son. He was supportive but I said, 'Gee, I don't know. College is a four-year commitment. In four years, I'll be seventy years old.' He said, 'Dad, how old will you be in four years if you *don't* go to college?' He had a point there.

"I didn't know if I could even make it in. I talked to the admission counselor. She said she'd need to see my high school transcripts. I said, 'Lady, my high school don't even exist no more! They shut it down back in the '80s.' Then she said she'd need to see my SAT. 'You want me to write an essay about tea?' 'No, no, the SAT. It's a test you take to get into college.'

"I didn't have that either. Fortunately, I learned the Chicago Archdiocese keeps permanent transcripts of all its students, so I sent a copy to the college. They must not have looked at them very hard because they let me in. Maybe they just needed my tuition money, I don't know. At any rate, in 2015, at the age of sixty six, I became a freshman at Fort Dearborn State University.

"I figured if I were going to do this, I needed to do it right. I was single, a widower, so I sold my house, gave most of my crap to my sons to hold onto for me, and moved into the dorm.

"Living in the dorm was great—for a year. But the dorm really isn't a place for an old guy like me, so after a year, I moved into an apartment. Still, that year in the dorm gave me my first lesson from college: Don't be afraid to ask for help.

"I brought a typewriter with me to college. I never owned a computer in my life. I was afraid of them. To me, a browser was a guy who went into a store and didn't buy anything. So, one night I'm typing up a paper. CLICK-CLICK-CLICK. And this guy, Dylan, comes into my room.

"Steve, what're you doing in here? You're driving me crazy next door."

"I'm typing up a paper."

"On that old thing? Nobody uses typewriters anymore. They use computers or their phones."

"Well, I don't know how to use a computer. Do you suppose you could teach me?"

"Sure!"

"Well, within a week, Dylan's got me completely functional on the computer machine. Now I'm like a tech addict. I'm texting, doing selfies, even Snapchatting with my grandkids. I love it and I owe it all to Dylan.

"People have a tendency to associate only with people who are similar to them. It's easy, it's comfortable, and it reinforces what we already believe. But when you step out of your comfort zone and associate with people who are different from you, different age, race, religion, social class, you learn from them. And they learn from you.

"When I hear people complain about 'kids these days', I ask 'Do you associate with kids these days? Cause I do, and I say our future looks brighter than ever.'

"When I was young, I never went to concerts. But guess what? At 67, I went to my first rock concert—Riot Fest. I had to take a few precautions before I went. Like, a three-hour nap that afternoon. On the other hand, I didn't need earplugs on account-a my hearing's already half shot. I gotta say, it wasn't bad! I mean, I couldn't slam dance or anything like that, but I had a good time. Which brings me to my second lesson: try new things.

"I spent most of my life doing the same things over and over. Get up, go to work, come home, watch TV, go to bed. Repeat. You hear the phrase, "life goes by fast when you get older?" Well, I disagree. I say life goes fast when you're stuck in a routine. But when you try new things, you challenge your body and your mind. You get caught up in the moment and each moment has deeper meaning.

"I didn't have perfect grades in college. I had my share of Cs. But I tell you what, I earned every one of those Cs, especially math. And that's my third lesson: If it doesn't challenge you, it doesn't change you.

"As an undergraduate, you have to take all sorts of classes in areas you wouldn't normally take. But now I understand so much more about the world because I took economics, sociology, world literature. Je parle en peu francais. I know the quadratic formula. I can tell you all about Nietzsche, and then explain to you why I think he was wrong. I can do all of this and more because I have had a diverse education.

"You know, there were advantages to being the oldest student on campus. I never got carded at the bars. History was easy. I lived through half of it. *Every* year was my senior year. I qualified for both the student *and* senior discounts. And if I wanted to smoke pot, I probably coulda gotten a prescription.

"It wasn't easy, but I did it. And when I look out on this graduating class, I see over two thousand other people who did it, even though it wasn't easy. I see single parents. I see people with disabilities. I see people who scrimped and saved to make their tuition payments. I see immigrants and I see the first people in their family to go to college.

"Fort Dearborn State University class of 2019, I congratulate you on your achievement. But remember: the educated never truly graduate!"

The crowd applauds. A handful of crowd members rise, suggesting to others they should rise, as well. Within seconds, the arena is awash in people standing, applauding Steve's magnificent speech.

Cornerstone

poetry by writers K-12

Kate Rowberry

DEIFIED TRIPTYCH

the grass will grow over
your feet if you hold still.
impossible when he tells
you to move on, to march
in rain boots. feel nature
settle over your skin. a
membrane. ascetic
accidents. don't crush the
flurry of petals that coat
the ground. there is always
more to do in the flesh.

the first sunset is organic
terror. he says not to worry
because the sun will rise
again. he means that we
will tug it back onto its
throne in the clouds
because we cannot
worship the moon. not
silver. the constellations
are coming unstuck so
watch for falling stars.
tomorrow is a threat
refracted as a promise.

darkness breathes loudest.
a colonnade of trunks
extends its boughs in an
eternal stretch. the
branches crack the moon
and snag the breeze,
ripping into the comforting
seams of dawn. harmony
finds itself swimming up a
scalloped waterfall. a leaf
cartwheels in the wind's
wake and you ask him
why this is earth. he has
misplaced his concern
after eden. transgression.

Faye Zhang

My Rabbit

Rabbit rush, cremator of riverside skulls
traipse through my fairy rings, my crushed duck-eggs
soft shells beneath your thoughtful feet
think some more, Rabbit, and Rabbit run
bank to bank, across ponderous streams
the water runs clear, and look! jagged rock,
Rabbit, watch out.
see the gravestone cattails, hear the
funeral dirge of thrush song
leap and don't look down, Rabbit.
quick on the gashed pads of your careful feet
the river is hungry, and i am waiting

i can taste your matted fur from the other side.

Jiayi Shao

DOOR KNOB

I am a door
knob, round,
painted in metallic silver, as if to coat
my indecision—
Some say I lack the resolution
of a handle, with
the absence of clean lines,
angles and edges.

But no, I simply
ask for more commitment,
An embrace of the whole hand
(that is too candid for some)
A direct acknowledgement—
You can't dismiss me with the nudge of an elbow.

I
lead to new worlds
that you can't await
to venture, so you
Embrace me with your whole hand,
Asking for a dance,
Covering your mottled reflection.

Emma Catherine Hoff

A Poem with Wings

This poem
had wings before
being trapped.

This poem was words
ricocheting across the sky
before it was written.

This poem was free
before
it flew through the burning
furnaces of thought.

"*Shhh*"
you told the bird
on wings of air.

"*Listen*"
you told the bird
perched on your shoulder.

"Confinement
in a room
will become your
own little world
and you will lean
into it,
your soul
will travel and there
will be no more monster,
just a flower,
a walk,
I see the color of your feathers,
I love it so."

Gentle curving of the beak,
the knife-like claws
that scraped
your enemies.

Please become
anew,
be the same,
but different,
my own,
I take you,
I feel you,
I want you,
I write you
down in my little book.

Yunzhong Mao

GHAZAL OF A SUMMER DAY

Find me an artifact to prove my existence.
Show me the mechanism of your soul.

There is a bird that lands on the twig.
Tree rooted, as a medieval guardian.

The wind finally leaves the ocean.
A lonely teenager, losing faith for being free.

The tenor have to cry in Latin.
Mozart's funeral consecrated, ages to come.

The Siberian iris does not know to close.
Its fragrance robbed by the mere presence of air.

Helena Wu

WORLD

"Our house is on fire" - burns a carmine world
"Our emperors are naked" - is your bottom bared to a latrine world?

Dust chokes forests and ash hammers us like hail
I'd drown you in gasoline for a chance at a green world

Winter is an iceberg that bleeds more every year
Would you cauterize it if the sea returns to a Pliocene world?

I imagine at 87, I'll be white haired like you
But your decisions have made my roots gray - and I'm only seventeen,
    world!

Go on - extinguish me, Helena, the shining light
The stars above will burn - until we have a clean world.

Mary Virginia Vietor

ARACHNE

Her web is spun with lucent wisps of filmy thought,
Twining from deft fingers like arpeggios
Loosed from the harpist's racing hands.
Dewdrops pearl upon the strands,
Their occasional iridescence glinting
Off her shattered shards of brilliancy.

Cursed by Athene, captive to a crisscrossed reverie
Of drifting diaphanous dreams,
She cannot cease constructing these concentric circles,
An architecture of arguments spiraling ever inward
To meet the one unpardonable paradox:
Profane divinity,
Ichor defiled with the mortal outrages of immortality.

And even yet, the echoes of adulation
Ringing through Olympian halls.

Cloris Shi

HERE I WRITE AN ELEGY TO YOU

so you remember how on those summer nights we read from our
guinness world records book the glossy silver cover like the mouth of
a whitefish we tilted up peered into & when we are tucking each sharp
corner into our belly buttons & folding our sticky hands praying the
fluttering night light wouldn't shine too brightly onto our empty covers
while we are on the rooftop slapping mayflies from bleached arms until
we fade into the night sky vitiligo foggy freckled with stars we are too
child to sleep through & we can only flip a couple of those sterile pages
a night chewing the gummy pictures filling our bellies a sweet cyst as we
are learning to spot the missing in this dewy mouth of the lonely how to
lure the awake & bait those lodged in the scaled throat & we are pressing
our palms onto the pages & cracking the raw spine open to collect the
moonshine we can & you remember how we are trying so hard to find
some new record to break & how your favorite thing was the world's
oldest people on the two-page spread & how you would run your fingers
on the liver spots on their ugly faces & when you said *i don't want to
live that long* i had said yeah and somehow then i had known you didn't
believe me which is to say don't you remember how i was counting the
years which you still needed then or the years you don't need now or how
god i don't want to believe you wanted to die

CONTRIBUTOR'S NOTES

V. Joshua Adams is a poet, scholar, translator, and critic. His debut full-length collection, *Past Lives*, will be published by JackLeg Press in 2024. Work of his has appeared recently or is forthcoming in *Allium, Painted Bride Quarterly, Bennington Review, Annulet, Chicago Review* and *The Los Angeles Review of Books*. He teaches at the University of Louisville.

Joseph G. Anthony moved in 1980 from Manhattan to Hazard, Kentucky. His most recent novel, *A Wounded Snake*, was reviewed and recommended by *US Review* as having "moments of lyrical wisdom and keen insight... The historical detail vividly imparts the legacy of racial struggle in America." *The Lexington Herald–Leader* described Anthony's previous novel, *Wanted: Good Family*, as "masterfully written and well-grounded in Kentucky history and mannerisms {exploring} race, class, relationship and the potential for change." Anthony's previous books include two short story collections, *Bluegrass Funeral* and *Camden Blues*, and two novels, *Peril, Kentucky*, and *Pickering's Mountain*. He has appeared in numerous publications including *Kentucky's Twelve Days of Christmas* and *The Kentucky Humanities Journal*.

Dianne Aprile is the author of four books, including a collaboration with the late Louisville artist Julius Friedman—an anthology of brief poems and prose and fine art photographs, titled *The Book*—and with Indiana printmaker Mary Lou Hess on *The Eye is Not Enough*. With a special interest in the intersection of words and visual imagery, Dianne has also collaborated with visual artists on book projects, gallery shows, Zoom classes and in-person workshops. After 13 years living in the Pacific Northwest, she and her husband Ken Shapero moved back to Louisville this month. She is the recipient of a Hedgebrook Women Writers Residency on Whidbey Island, a Washington State Artist Trust Fellowship and was one of 12 Pacific Northwest writers selected in 2019 for Jack Straw Writers Program. She has received fellowships, grants, awards and residencies from the Kentucky Foundation for Women, the Kentucky Arts Council, the National Society of Newspaper Columnists, the Society of Professional Journalists and others. Her poetry and essays have appeared in anthologies, journals, and in newspapers, including an essay on living in Kirkland, WA, the site of the first major outbreak of Covid-19 in the US. She was twice nominated for a Pushcart, both times with excerpts from her memoir in progress. During her 30-year career as a journalist, she was a Sunday columnist, an arts writer/reviewer and part of a *The Courier-Journal* team that won a staff Pulitzer Prize in 1989. She was also co-owner of a downtown Louisville jazz club, The Jazz Factory, with her husband for five years. Since its inception in 2001, Dianne has served on the faculty of Spalding University's Naslund-Mann School of Writing.

Daisy Bassen is a poet and child psychiatrist who graduated from Princeton University's Creative Writing Program and completed her medical training at The University of Rochester and Brown. Her work has been published in *Salamander, McSweeney's, Smartish Pace, Crab Creek Review*, and *[PANK]* among other journals. She was the winner of the

So to Speak 2019 Poetry Contest, the 2019 ILDS White Mice Contest, the 2020 Beullah Rose Poetry Prize, and the 2022 Erskine J Poetry Prize. She was doubly nominated for the 2019 and 2021 Best of the Net Anthology and for a 2019 and 2020 Pushcart Prize. She lives in Rhode Island with her family.

Elya Braden is the author of the chapbooks *Open The Fist*, released in 2020, and *The Sight of Invisible Longing*, coming out in 2023, both by Finishing Line Press. She is a writer and mixed-media artist living in Ventura County, CA, and is Assistant Editor of *Gyroscope Review*. Her work has been widely published, and her poems have received a Pushcart Prize nomination and several Best of the Net nominations. www.elyabraden.com.

Gaylord Brewer is a professor at Middle Tennessee State University, where he founded and for 20+ years edited the journal *Poems & Plays*. The most recent of his sixteen books of poetry, fiction, criticism, and cookery are two collections of poems, *The Feral Condition* (Negative Capability, 2018) and *Worship the Pig* (Red Hen, 2020). A volume of short creative nonfiction, *Before the Storm Takes It Away*, is forthcoming from Red Hen in spring 2024.

Mary Buchinger is the author of five poetry collections, including /klaudz/ (2021), *e i n f ü h l u n g/in feeling* (2018), and *VIROLOGY* (forthcoming). She serves on the New England Poetry Club board and teaches at the Massachusetts College of Pharmacy and Health Sciences in Boston.

Wendy Taylor Carlisle lives in the Arkansas Ozarks. She is the author of four books and five chapbooks and is the 2020 winner of the Phillip H. McMath Post-Publication Award for *The Mercy of Traffic*. Find more of her work at www.wendytaylorcarlisle.com.

Bob Chikos lives in Cary, Illinois, but in his mind, he is in 1970s southern California, where most of his favorite TV shows take place. He hopes to someday outsmart Columbo.

Matt Dennison is the author of *Kind Surgery*, from Urtica Press (Fr.) and *Waiting for Better*, from Main Street Rag Press. His work has appeared in *Verse Daily, Rattle, Bayou Magazine, Redivider, Natural Bridge, The Spoon River Poetry Review* and *Cider Press Review*, among others. He has also made short films with Michael Dickes, Swoon, Marie Craven and Jutta Pryor.

Denise Duhamel's most recent books of poetry are *Second Story* (Pittsburgh, 2021) and *Scald* (2017). *Blowout* (2013) was a finalist for the National Book Critics Circle Award. As a former contributor, an essay she co-wrote with Julie Marie Wade ("22 Firsts") appeared in *The Louisville Review* in 2015. A recipient of fellowships from the Guggenheim Foundation and the National Endowment for the Arts, she teaches at Florida International University in Miami.

In 1983, **Millard Dunn** won the chapbook contest sponsored by the Kentucky Arts

Council and Kentucky Department for Libraries and Archives. His chapbook, *Engraved on Air*, was published in that year. His collection of poems *Places We Could Never Find Alone* was published in 2011 by The Ink Brush Press of Temple, Texas. He has published poems in *The Concho River Review, Film and History, Hard Scuffle Folio, The IUS Review, Jam To-Day, Kansas Quarterly, The Louisville Review, New North Carolina Poetry: The Eighties, The Ohio Review, Poetry Northwest, The Sandhills St. Andrews Review, Southern Poetry Review*, and *this end up postcards.*

Michelle Bonczek Evory is the author of *The Ghosts of Lost Animals*, winner of the Barry Spacks Award and a 2021 Independent Publisher Book Award. Her open-source book *Naming the Unnameable: An Approach to Poetry for New Generations* (Open SUNY Textbooks) is taught in creative writing courses throughout the world. She is a creative writing instructor and mentor at The Poet's Billow and can be found at www.michellebonczekevory.com.

Patricia Foster is the author of *All the Lost Girls* (PEN/Jerard Award), *Just beneath My Skin* (essays), *Girl from Soldier Creek* (SFA Novel Award), a forthcoming collection, *Written in the Sky*, and the editor of four anthologies, most recently, *Understanding the Essay* (with Jeff Porter). She has received a Pushcart Prize, a Clarence Cason Award, a Theodore Hoepfner Award, a Dean's Scholar Award, a Yaddo Fellowship, a Carl Klaus Teaching Award, and sixteen Notables in the *Best American Essays* series. She has been a juror for the Windham-Campbell Literature Prize in Nonfiction (Yale) and a fellow at the Inaugural Writing Residency at Sun Yat-sen University. She has been a professor in the MFA Program in Nonfiction at the University of Iowa for over twenty-three years and has taught writing in France, Australia, Italy, the Czech Republic, and Spain.

Renee Gilmore writes about her experiences growing up in a small town in the Midwest, and fearlessly explores the illusion of happiness. She identifies as a person with a disability. She received her bachelor's degree from the University of New Mexico, and her master's degree from Hamline University. Her poems have appeared or are upcoming in *Of Rust and Glass, Eastern Iowa Review, The Raven Review*, and *Peauxdunque Review.*

Michael J. Galko is a scientist and poet who lives and works in Houston, Texas. He was a 2019 Pushcart Award nominee and a finalist in the 2020 *Naugatuck River Review* narrative poetry contest. In the past year he has had poems published or accepted at *Talking River Review, Burningword Literary Journal, Gargoyle, Lullwater Review, Sierra Nevada Review, Jersey Devil Press*, and *The Paterson Literary Review*, among other journals.

Michelle Glans recently received her Bachelor's Degree from Washington University in St. Louis, where she studied Biomedical Engineering and writing. Her poems have been featured in the *Young American Poetry Digest, Orange Island Review, Odet Literary Journal* and *SWWIM Every Day*. She has won the Ringling College of Art and Design "Storytellers of Tomorrow" Competition, Austin International Poetry Festival Competition, and the It's All Write Short Story Competition. Michelle currently resides in in Madison, Wisconsin, with her cat Benjamin.

Lynn Gordon is a past contributor to *The Louisville Review*; her fiction has also appeared in *The Southampton Review, Epiphany, Baltimore Review, Ruminate, Zone 3*, and other journals. Lynn lives in Northern California.

Jeff Hardin is the author of seven collections of poetry, most recently *Watermark, A Clearing Space in the Middle of Being*, and *No Other Kind of World*. His work has received the Nicholas Roerich Prize, the Donald Justice Prize, and the X. J. Kennedy Prize. Recent and forthcoming poems appear in *Zone 3, The Laurel Review, Literary Matters, Braided Way, Southern Poetry Review*, and *The Los Angeles Review*. He lives and teaches in TN.

Marcia L. Hurlow is professor emeritus of creative writing, journalism and TESOL at Asbury University. Her first full-length collection of poetry, *Anomie*, won the Edges Prize at WordTech, and she has also published five chapbooks. She has won the Al Smith Fellowship in Poetry twice and currently serves as co-editor of *Kansas City Voices*.

Donald Illich has published poems in journals such as *Iowa Review, Okay Donkey*, and *Nimrod*. He lives in Rockville, Maryland.

Marianne Kunkel is the author of *Hillary, Made Up* (Stephen F. Austin State University Press) and *The Laughing Game* (Finishing Line Press), as well as poems that have appeared in *The Missouri Review, The Notre Dame Review, Hayden's Ferry Review, Rattle*, and elsewhere. Marianne is an Assistant Professor of English at Johnson County Community College in the Kansas City, Missouri, area. While earning her Ph.D. at the University of Nebraska-Lincoln, she was the managing editor of *Prairie Schooner* and the African Poetry Book Fund. She's currently the co-editor-in-chief of *Kansas City Voices* and *Kansas City Voices Youth*.

Jody Lisberger's stories have been published in *Fugue, Michigan Quarterly Review, Confrontation, The Louisville Review, Timberline Review*, and *Jabberwock Review*, among others, and have also won prizes at *Quarterly West* (3rd), *American Literary Review* (finalist), and *Sequestrum* (finalist). Her 2008 story collection *Remember Love* was nominated for a National Book Award. Two of her stories have been nominated for Pushcarts. She has a Ph.D. in English and an M.F.A. in Writing (Vermont College). She lives in Rhode Island.

Congxia Ma 马丛霞 holds a Master of Fine Arts degree from the Central Academy of Fine Arts in Beijing and is a lecturer of fine arts at the Henan Normal University, Henan Province, China. She has exhibited her artwork widely throughout China and has published essays on the arts and criticism. With the support of a China National Fellowship, Ma is currently spending her one-year sabbatical in the United States to conduct research projects on contemporary art and education as a visiting scholar at the University of Louisville, hosted by the Department of Art and Design.

Angie Macri is the author of *Sunset Cue* (Bordighera), winner of the Lauria/Frasca Poetry Prize, and *Underwater Panther* (Southeast Missouri State University), winner of the Cowles Poetry Book Prize. An Arkansas Arts Council fellow, she lives in Hot Springs and teaches at Hendrix College.

Melissa Madenski lived for thirty-five years at the edge of the Siuslaw Forest in Oregon, where she and her children walked headlands and paddled coastal rivers and streams. Her poetry and essays have appeared in journals, anthologies, and a chapbook, *Endurance*. She writes and teaches now from her birthplace in Portland, Oregon.

Josh Mahler lives and writes in Virginia. His poems have appeared or are forthcoming in *The Southern Poetry Anthology, Vol. IX: Virginia*, from Texas Review Press, *South Dakota Review*, *The Adirondack Review*, *The Carolina Quarterly*, *The Comstock Review*, *Bodega*, *Exit 7*, *Puerto del Sol*, and elsewhere.

Sarah Martin teaches photography and digital media and is currently the chair of Bellarmine University's Art Department. Sarah earned her BA in Media Art from the University of Tennessee and her MFA in Photography from Yale University. Prior to teaching at Bellarmine University, Sarah taught at Yale University, The University of Tennessee, created a photography major at the University of North Carolina at Greensboro and served as Artist in Residence for a year at Lyon College. Sarah exhibits her photography and video art internationally; you can view her work at www.thesarahmartin.com.

Juan Pablo Mobili was born in Buenos Aires and adopted by New York. His poems appeared in *The American Journal of Poetry*, *The Worcester Review*, *Otoliths* (Australia) *Impspired* (UK), and *Bosphorus Review of Books* (Turkey) among others. His work received an Honorable Mention from the International Human Rights Art Festival, and nominations for the Pushcart Prize and the Best of the Net, in 2020 and 2021. His chapbook, "Contraband," was published this year.

Southern poet **Karen McAferty Morris** writes about nature and social issues. Her poetry has been recognized for its "appeal to the senses, the intellect, and the imagination." Her poetry collections *Elemental* (2018), *Confluence* (2020) and *Significance: Poems of Small Encounters*, (2022) are national prize winners. She lives in the Florida Panhandle.

James B. Nicola's poems have appeared in the *Antioch*, *Southwest* and *Atlanta Reviews*; *Rattle*; and *Barrow Street*. His seven full-length collections (2014-22) are *Manhattan Plaza*, *Stage to Page*, *Wind in the Cave*, *Out of Nothing*, *Quickening*, *Fires of Heaven*, and *Turns & Twists* (just out). His nonfiction book *Playing the Audience* won a Choice award. His poetry has received a Dana Literary Award, two Willow Review awards, Storyteller's People's Choice award, one Best of Net nomination, and eight Pushcart noms—for which he feels both stunned and grateful. A Yale grad, he hosts the Hell's Kitchen International Writers' Round Table at his library branch in Manhattan: walk-ins welcome.

John A. Nieves has poems forthcoming or recently published in journals such as: *North American Review, Copper Nickel, 32 Poems, American Literary Review* and *Massachusetts Review.* He won the Indiana Review Poetry Contest and his first book, *Curio,* won the Elixir Press Annual Poetry Award Judge's Prize. He is associate professor of English at Salisbury University and an editor of *The Shore Poetry.* He received his MA from University of South Florida and his PhD from the University of Missouri.

An English professor, Methodist pastor, clarinetist, and poet, **Rosanne Osborne** holds the Ph.D. in English from the University of Alabama, the MFA from Spalding University, and the MRE and MDiv from New Orleans Baptist Theological Seminary. She grew up in Missouri but has lived most of her adult life in Louisiana. Her work has appeared in *Tar River Poetry, Alabama Review, Christian Century, Ruminate, Thema, Penwood Review, The Village Pariah,* and several other journals. *Tapestry of Counterpoint,* a chapbook of poems, is forthcoming from Finishing Line Press.

Tony O'Keeffe is a long-term resident of Louisville who flees in summer to northern Michigan.

Pat Owen is the author of three collections of poetry. *Crossing the Sky Bridge* was published by Larkspur Press in 2016 and *Orion's Belt at the End of the Drive* and *Bardo of Becoming* were published by Accents Publisher in 2019 and 2022 respectively.

Jeremy Paden is professor of Latin American literature at Transylvania University and on faculty at Spalding's Sena Jeter Naslund-Karen Mann Graduate School of Writing where he mentors in literary translation. He is the author of three chapbooks of poems, one illustrated children's book, and two full-length collections. He is also the Spanish to English translator of one chapbook of poems and three full-length collections. *Under the Ocelot Sun* (Shadelandhouse Modern Press, 2020), a bilingual illustrated children's book about the Central American migrant caravans, won an Campoy-Ada prize for Spanish language children's books. His most current books are *world as sacred burning heart* (3: A Taos Press, 2021) and *Self-Portrait as an Iguana* (Valparaíso USA, 2021). *Self-Portrait,* a bilingual collection of poems written in Spanish and translated to English, co-won the first Poeta en Nueva York Prize.

John Repp is a poet and fiction writer living in Erie, Pennsylvania. His most recent book is *The Soul of Rock & Roll: Poems Acoustic, Electric & Remixed, 1980-2020,* published by Broadstone Books.

Mrinal Rajaram is an independent writer from Chennai, India. His fiction has appeared online and in print in *The Madras Mag, The Madras Mag Anthology Of Contemporary Writing,* Sahitya Akademi's *Indian Literature, The Bombay Review* and *Five on the Fifth.* His nonfiction may be accessed from the pages of *The Times of India, The Economic Times, The New Indian Express, Firstpost* and *Silverscreen.* He was longlisted for *The Bombay Review*'s inaugural Creative Writing Awards for Fiction in 2021. Mrinal is in the process of seeking out agents and publishers interested in his first collection of stories.

Chris Reitz is director of the Hite Institute for Art and Design at the University of Louisville, where he is also Assistant Professor of Critical and Curatorial Studies and Gallery Director. His writing on art and culture has appeared in *October, The Baffler,* and *Texte zur Kunst* among many other venues. His first book, *Martin Kippenberger: Everything is Everywhere*, is forthcoming from MIT Press.

Diane Scholl is Professor Emerita of English at Luther College in Decorah, Iowa, where she's taught American and modern British literature, poetry courses, and literature by women. Her poems have been published by *Louisville Review, Cider Press Review, Sow's Ear Poetry Review, Cold Mountain Review*, and *Ruminate*, among other places. More poems are forthcoming in *Spoon River Poetry Review*. In 2019, her chapbook, *Salt*, was published by Seven Kitchens Press. When she's not writing she enjoys hiking and biking among the scenic bluffs of NE Iowa, and reading mysteries, a poet's food.

Joe Schmidt (aka the hiker "Triton") is an instructor of English in the School of Foreign Languages at Gaziantep University, in Turkey. He was educated at Western Kentucky University, the University of Louisville, and Spalding University. A native of Staten Island in New York City, he is a husband, a father, and a citizen of the world.

Elizabeth Schoettle was born in Bryn Mawr, Pennsylvania. She studied at Gettysburg College for two years before transferring to Hunter College, where she graduated with a BA in film production. She currently lives in NYC as a full-time artist and writer. She is also the subject of a docu-series about her life as an artist. She has been published multiple times on Mr. Beller's Neighborhood (website).

Lana Spendl is the author of the chapbook *We Cradled Each Other in the Air*. Her work has appeared in *The Rumpus, Hobart, The Greensboro Review, Notre Dame Review, New Ohio Review, Epiphany, Zone 3*, and other journals. She is a refugee from the Bosnian War in the '90s, and her childhood was divided between Bosnia and Spain prior to her family's move to the States.

Robert Eric Shoemaker is a poet and interdisciplinary artist. Eric holds a PhD in Humanities from the University of Louisville and an MFA in Creative Writing & Poetics from Naropa University. Eric works in magical poetics, queer theory and poetry, public history, translation, and gender and sexuality. Eric has released three books: *Ca'Venezia* (2021), *We Knew No Mortality* (2018), and *30 Days Dry* (2015). Other work has been seen with *Rattle, Transom, Plath Profiles, Signs and Society, Asymptote, Jacket2, Entropy, Gender Forum, Exchanges, Columbia Journal, Bombay Gin*, and others. Eric is the Digital Archive Editor at the Poetry Foundation. Follow him at reshoemaker.com and find him on social media @Robert.E.Shoe.

Ciara Shuttleworth is the author of *Rabbit Heart, Night Holds Its Own*, and the gonzo prose book *4,500 Miles: Taking Jack Back On the Road.* She has published in journals and anthologies including *The Norton Anthology of Literature* and *The New Yorker.* She lives in California.

Costa Rican-American **Mark Smith-Soto** has authored four prize-winning chapbooks and three full-length poetry collections, *Our Lives Are Rivers* (University Press of Florida, 2003), *Any Second Now* (Main Street Rag Publishing Co., 2006) and *Time Pieces* (Main Street Rag Publishing Co., 2015). His work has appeared in *The Bitter Oleander, Kenyon Review, Literary Review, Louisville Review; Nimrod, Poetry East, Rattle, The Sun* and many other publications and been nominated several times for a Pushcart Prize. In 2006 he was recognized with an NEA Fellowship in Creative Writing. His book of translations *Fever Season: Selected Poetry of Ana Istarú* (2010) and his lyrical memoir *Berkeley Prelude* (2013) were both published by Unicorn Press.

Chelsie Taylor lives in Springfield, Kentucky, with her husband and son. Her work has been previously published in *Poetry East* and *The Louisville Review.*

Rebecca Thrush works in property management in Massachusetts. Poetry and digital mixed media help her better understand nature and interpersonal relationships. Select pieces have appeared in *86 Logic* and *Coffee People Zine*, as well as across a variety of other print and online publications. Find out more on Instagram @rebeleigh92.

Catherine Uroff's short fiction has appeared (or is forthcoming) in a variety of literary journals, including *Oyster River Pages, Faultline, Sou'wester, Beloit Fiction Journal, Hobart, Prairie Schooner, Valparaiso Fiction Review, Bellevue Literary Review*, and *The Roanoke Review.* She is a past recipient of the Prairie Schooner Glenna Luschei Award. In addition, her short fiction has been awarded Honorable Mention in the Craft Literary Short Story Contest and I've been a finalist in American Short Fiction's short story contest. Uroff was recently honored as a semi-finalist in OSU's The Journal 2022 Non/Fiction Collection Prize for her short story collection.

Luke Wallin's books include eight novels for children and young adults, and works on conservation writing. With his daughter Eva Sage Gordon, Luke wrote *The Everything Guide to Writing Children's Books*, 2nd edition. Luke is Professor Emeritus at the University of Massachusetts Dartmouth and taught for 12 years in Spalding's MFA in Writing program. A 2021 reading and interview appear on YouTube at Moon Views Episode 1: Luke Wallin Interview. Luke's essay, "Longing for Wilderness," will appear in the Fall 2022 issue of the magazine *Sisyphus*, online. His poem "White Oaks" appears in the 2022 Fall Equinox issue of *Canary* magazine, online.

David Wilde currently lives and works in the City of San Francisco. He dabbles in fiction on the occasion and enjoys experiencing the world through his characters. He believes there's a strong kind of empathy/wisdom that comes from seeing life through varying viewpoints. "Truth is the sum of all perspectives," the wise man once said. David has recently been published in *Fiction International* (short story), and has two self-published books to his name.

Kristin Camitta Zimet is a poet, visual artist, and naturalist in the Shenandoah Valley of Virginia. Her poetry is in hundreds of journals in seven countries. She is the editor of *The Sow's Ear Poetry Review* and the author of a collection of poems, *Take in My Arms the Dark.*

CORNERSTONE CONTRIBUTOR'S NOTES

Emma Catherine Hoff is ten years old and a student at PS24 in the Bronx, NYC. Her poems, essays, and book reviews have appeared in *The Louisville Review, Rattle Young Poets Anthology, Stone Soup Magazine,* and the *Stone Soup Blog.* Her poetry collection, *The Immortal Jellyfish,* was a finalist for the 2021 Stone Soup Book Contest. When not reading and writing, Emma likes to sing, play piano, hang out with her cat, Gavroche, and play board games.

Yunzhong Mao is a high school junior student at Concord Academy. His work has been recognized by the Scholastics Art & Writing Awards. He enjoys reading and writing poetry, as well as learning about philosophy. He is also an avid listener to jazz and classical music. His favorite writers include Louise Glück, Haruki Murakami, and Jhumpa Lahiri.

Kate Rowberry is a writer who is inspired by words she encounters, scenarios she imagines, and events she lives through. Her work has appeared in *The Global Youth Review* and *Paper Crane Journal* and has been recognized by the Alliance for Young Artists & Writers and the Bow Seat Ocean Awareness Contest. Reading is also one of her favorite activities, but she may be guilty of tsundoku. That TBR list must end somewhere, right?

Jiayi Shao is a high school senior in Toronto, Canada. Her previous work has been recognized by *The Louisville Review, TeenInk,* the *IHRAF Youth Speaks* anthology, among others. She has an intrinsic curiosity that has guided her to so many unique experiences and fascinating exchanges in life. At present, she is also mildly complacent at the fact that she sees the elusive beauty in life and has the ability to communicate it through the vessel of words and poetry.

Cloris Shi is a poet from southern California. Her work is published or forthcoming in *Eunoia Review, Alliance for Young Artists & Writers, BreakBread Literature, Élan Magazine, The Foredge Review,* and other places. You can find her on Twitter at @ClorisShi, where she tweets about poetry.

Mary Virginia Vietor is a high school senior from Phoenix, Arizona. She enjoys playing the harp, writing, painting, and taking long walks with her corgi. Her work has previously appeared on the Dappled Things literary blog.

Helena Wu is a student living in Los Angeles. She enjoys swimming, traveling the world with her family and playing music. Helena considers her family and friends to be most important to her. If she isn't in an orchestra rehearsal, one can find her writing poetry.

Faye Zhang is a rising senior at Eastview High School in Minnesota. She enjoys reading, writing, and climbing in her spare time. Her favorite authors are Neil Gaiman and Salman Rushdie.

ABOUT THE COVER ARTIST

Ying Kit Chan is a Chinese American artist who was born in Hong Kong. For four decades, Chan has used his art projects to celebrate the beauty of nature, but also to critique the anthropogenic impact on the environment. Serving as a professor of art at the University of Louisville for over three decades, Chan continues to integrate his professional pursuit with his teaching. As demonstrated by the span and breadth of his work, his consistent thematic focus on nature has produced a bounty of artistic materials, concepts, and cultural insights. Chan has presented his artwork in over 200 exhibitions in the United States as well as in Australia, Canada, Ecuador, Germany, Italy, Korea, Japan, England, Hong Kong, Poland, Switzerland, Taiwan, and Portugal. He is currently the Director of Graduate Studies in Art and Design at the University of Louisville.

CPSIA information can be obtained
at www.ICGtesting.com
Printed in the USA
JSHW020438310123
37104JS00004B/23